TO

_____

FROM

_____

DATE

_____

# DESIGNED
## — FOR —
# GREATNESS

### DEVOTIONS
### FOR MEN

DaySpring

LIVE YOUR FAITH

*Designed for Greatness: Devotions for Men*

First Edition, November 2022

Published by:

2115A Highway 16 East
Siloam Springs, AR 72761
dayspring.com

Written with the assistance of: Peachtree Publishing Services

Cover Design by: Hannah Bedell

Printed in Canada
Prime: J9334
ISBN: 978-1-64870-845-9

# CONTENTS

# GOD OF HOPE

*I pray that God, the source of hope,*
*will fill you completely with joy and peace*
*because you trust in Him.*
*Then you will overflow with confident hope*
*through the power of the Holy Spirit.*

ROMANS 15:13 NLT

It may be a financial reversal, or a temptation you've given in to, or a disappointment in relationships. On those days when life delivers a sucker punch to your soul and you wonder if you can ever be hopeful again, God delivers a sucker punch to your hopelessness. "Remember Me, the God of hope!"

Our source of hope is the Creator of hope, not the twists and turns of life. You can count on life to ambush you when you least expect it, but God is waiting with an overflowing measure of hope at the perfect time. It is for us to believe Him and receive this hope.

As we trust in Him, He fills us with joy and peace. This is not because our life circumstances have changed; it is because our faithful God never changes and He overwhelms us with His presence. It may not necessarily be a feeling, but there is an unmistakable joy and peace resulting in hope for our soul.

Our mistake is putting our hope in the wrong place: in a promotion at work, in a gift of healing, in an apology from our spouse. We will no doubt be surprised one day to learn that God moved some of the puzzle pieces around to teach us not to depend on those solutions but rather to depend solely on Him. This is not cruelty on His part, but rather a saving grace!

### PRAYER:

*Father, forgive me for trying to solve my hopelessness by artificial means instead of being sustained by Your faithful arms. Rescue me from the hopelessness of life and fill me once again with Your joy, peace, and abiding hope. In Jesus' name, amen.*

# GREATNESS REDEFINED

*Samson . . . grew and the Lord blessed him,*
*and the Spirit of the Lord began to stir him.*

**JUDGES 13:24–25 NIV**

Judges 13:1 says that "the Israelites did evil in the eyes of the Lord, so the Lord delivered them into the hands of the Philistines for forty years." But God had a plan to deliver His people from their suffering, and that plan involved Samson.

An angel sent from God announced Samson's forthcoming birth not once but twice! Samson was miraculously conceived—the Bible tells us his mother was barren. God appointed Samson to be a judge over Israel, and the Spirit of God filled him, giving him supernatural strength. Samson was the strongest man in Israel, and surely the strongest man on earth.

All these details surrounding Samson's conception, strength, and God-given purpose must qualify him as a man of greatness. Even the writer of Hebrews included Samson in his list of great heroes of the faith (see Hebrews chapter 11).

If this was all we knew about Samson, it would be enough to call him great. Yet we find out later in the book of Judges that Samson was a womanizer, an angry man, and a murderer. So how can we consider him "great"?

Greatness doesn't come from being the best at something, or the strongest, or the smartest. Greatness comes by having *faith*. The rest of Samson's story is about God's humbling of Samson and Samson's final act of faith. He ended up getting his head shaved, losing his strength, having his eyes gouged out, and being paraded as a weak prisoner in front of thousands of Philistines. But in his most humiliating moment, he showed his true greatness through his faith in God. He cried out to his God, took hold of the supporting pillars in the banquet hall, and brought the building crashing down on his enemies, killing them all, including himself.

How are you pursuing greatness? In what are you putting your trust? We all have the possibility of achieving greatness, not from anything we do, but from putting our faith in the One who can do anything through us.

### PRAYER:

*Lord, please help me to trust in You with all my heart, all my mind, and all my strength. Help my faith in You to grow. I want to trust You just as Samson did at the end of his life. In Jesus' name, amen.*

# THE IMPORTANCE OF REMEMBERING

*For the one who lacks these qualities is blind or short-sighted, having forgotten his purification from his former sins.*

II PETER 1:9 NASB

Although the people closest to us might never forget, we would probably like to forget those times when an anniversary or an important event just happened to slip our minds. We don't mean to forget important dates and details— but the belated flowers don't help much.

Moving forward in a relationship is challenging when we drag that kind of weight behind us. It's also difficult to move forward in our relationship with God when we drag more serious weights behind us. When we ask God for His forgiveness and repent of our sin, He forgives us. But so often we seem to forget that He's forgiven us for those sins—and we hold on to guilt and shame.

When we forget God's forgiveness, we insult what He

did for us through Jesus' death on the cross. We say it wasn't enough for us and that our sin was too much for the blood of Jesus to cover. We pile the guilt on ourselves and stay buried in it—rather than receiving God's forgiveness and moving forward in victory.

God appointed the apostle Peter to remind us how we must remember that we are forgiven. Peter certainly was no stranger to sin. He denied knowing Jesus three times! Forgetting how he denied Jesus certainly wasn't easy for Peter. But Jesus forgave him, and accepting and remembering this forgiveness allowed Peter to continue forward as a follower of Jesus. God's Spirit inspired him to tell us not to forget our forgiveness. God wants to write this truth on our hearts.

We can't move forward in our relationship with God when we forget that He has forgiven us and what it cost Jesus to give us freedom from the guilt of our past.

### PRAYER:

*Father, forgive me for so easily forgetting how much You have forgiven me. Thank You that there is nothing left for us to add to Your grace. Help me to receive Your forgiveness, remember it, and move forward in living for You. In Jesus' name, amen.*

# THE PAST IS PAST

*I am convinced that neither death, nor life, nor angels,
nor principalities, nor things present, nor things to come,
nor powers, nor height, nor depth, nor any other created thing
will be able to separate us from the love of God
that is in Christ Jesus our Lord.*

**ROMANS 8:38–39 NASB**

These verses from the book of Romans are a powerful promise from God. In Paul's comprehensive list of things or persons that might try to separate us from God's love, he concludes with "Nor any other created thing." He writes this in case he has forgotten something.

Paul tells us that nothing in the present or the future can separate us from God's love. But why doesn't he include the past?

For believers, God promises that our past sins are not only forgiven but also forgotten. The past is past—over and done with. If this is how God sees it, who are we to tell Him it's just too good to believe?

Sadly, we often get stuck in the past by dwelling on

old habits, failed New Year's resolutions, broken hearts, humiliating mistakes. We struggle to accept God's love for us and believe the lie that we will never be good enough. How freeing it is for us not only to hear God's words but also to believe them! Through Christ, we are loved by God. And nothing—not anything in our present or in our future—will separate us from His love!

No sin or failure in our past can hold us back from moving forward in the love of God today. The Bible tells us, "If we confess our sins, He is faithful and righteous, so that He will forgive us our sins and cleanse us from all unrighteousness" (I John 1:9 NASB).

We can believe God or believe the lie. It is our daily choice. God wants us to believe the past is past, that He has forgiven us, and that He loves us.

### PRAYER:

*Forgive me, Father, for trusting a lie rather than trusting You. I too often dwell on past regrets and cheat myself of the present joy I have in Christ. Thank You for Your great and true promises. In Jesus' name, amen.*

# MORE THAN CONQUERORS

*No, in all these things we are more than conquerors through Him who loved us.*

**ROMANS 8:37 NIV**

**W**hen you hear the word *conquer*, what do you immediately think about? Maybe you think about how you finally "conquered" the enormous task of cleaning out your garage, or you came face-to-face with a fear and survived, or you landed a promotion, or you *finally* lost those last ten pounds. Or perhaps the word makes you think of wars or superheroes or your favorite football team's big win.

The English word *conquer* is translated from the Greek word *nikos*. (Fun fact: This is where the Nike company gets its name.) Paul uses the word *conquerors* in Romans 8:37 to encourage Christians who are suffering because of their faith. When Jesus speaks to the seven churches in Revelation 2–3, He uses the same word, which is translated as "one who is victorious." Jesus promises eternal blessings to those who are steadfast—who are victorious—in following Him.

When it comes to your relationship with God, do you think of yourself as a conqueror, as someone who has victory? Sure, there will be days when you have setbacks, when you get knocked off your feet and need some encouragement and reassurance to get back up. But if you keep your eyes on Jesus and on His promises for you, you are more than a conqueror. You have the Creator of the universe on your side! Because of His love for you, you can move forward. You can overcome the setbacks and struggles. You are not a failure.

God designed us to conquer, and our faith in Christ equips us for this task. We are not wimps. Those of us who belong to God because of our faith in Jesus and the victory that He has already accomplished through His death and resurrection are empowered by Him to win in this life.

### PRAYER:

*How good it is to imagine You smiling over my faith, Lord. I am more than a conqueror because of You. I march in this broken, fallen world as a winner, not a loser. Praise be to You. In Jesus' name, amen.*

# HUMILITY

*Now the man Moses was very humble,*
*more than any person who was on the face of the earth.*

**NUMBERS 12:3 NASB**

What do we know about Moses?

Moses floated in the Nile River in a basket, was adopted as Pharaoh's grandson, killed an Egyptian because he was beating a Hebrew slave, and spent forty years in the wilderness running for his life from Pharaoh. Then, he saw a burning bush, and God sent him back to Egypt to tell Pharaoh to let God's people go.

Using Moses as His instrument, God sent ten plagues on Egypt, parted the Red Sea, gave Moses the Ten Commandments, called water from a rock, and sent manna from heaven to feed millions of Israelites.

After all this, Moses led the Israelites to the border of the Promised Land, but he died before entering because he disobeyed God along the way. Moses was considered the greatest prophet in Israel's history, but why? If we want to accurately describe Moses, we would do well to read Numbers 12.

Most men might be less than thrilled with God's description of Moses as humble. We might prefer words like "great leader," "fearless," or "mighty in battle." Yet God calls him the humblest man on earth.

The context for this declaration is a complaint from Miriam (Moses' big sister) and Aaron (their brother). They decided Moses shouldn't be the rock star. They wanted some power for themselves. God heard them and told them to meet Him in the tabernacle. There, God informed them that they had no business speaking out against Moses, who was clearly chosen by God to lead the people of Israel. A cloud engulfed Miriam and Aaron. When it lifted, leprosy had turned Miriam as white as snow. We can only imagine how angry God was. Aaron begged Moses to ask God to heal her.

God defended Moses, but not because of anything great Moses had accomplished. He praised Moses for his humility. We must redefine *greatness* so it matches God's definition, not ours—and God thinks humility is great.

If we want to be great like Moses, we must be humble.

### PRAYER:

*Father, You have given us another look at the ways a man may be great. I ask for this kind of humility. In Jesus' name, amen.*

# WRESTLING WITH GOD

*And he said to him, "What is your name?" And he said, "Jacob."*
*Then he said, "Your name shall no longer be called Jacob,*
*but Israel, for you have striven with God and with men,*
*and have prevailed."*

GENESIS 32:27–28 ESV

The book of Genesis retells the details of an hours-long epic wrestling match. All night, Jacob wrestled with a man, and Jacob wouldn't let go—even when the man "touched his hip socket, and Jacob's hip was put out of joint" (Genesis 32:25). Jacob continued to hold on and asked for a blessing. The man proceeded to give Jacob a new name, because he had "striven with God and . . . prevailed." It turned out that the "man" was God Himself!

It seems unimaginable to us that Jacob wouldn't quit wrestling with a stranger even after suffering an injury. How often do we feel like quitting when things don't go our way or when we are hurt physically, mentally, or emotionally? We just can't keep going. The end seems nowhere in sight, and we wonder if God notices or even cares.

How surprised we would be if God pulled back the curtain of our fears and doubts and showed us Himself. He has been wrestling *with* us in our confusion and doubt. He has never for a moment abandoned us but rather is growing our faith through life's pain and uncertainty.

One thing is always true about wrestling: When the match begins, there's no question about who the opponent is. In this wrestling match in Genesis, Jacob didn't know the identity of his opponent until the match was over. Jacob called the place where the match occurred "Penial," which means "the face of God." He had seen God and lived to talk about it.

Our faith doesn't tend to grow when life is easy, predictable, and controllable. It grows in the midst of a struggle. And if we hold on to God—even if we can't see Him like Jacob did—the fight is always worth it.

### PRAYER:

*Father, thank You for sticking with me in the fight.*
*Please help me to persevere and not quit. Thank You*
*for reminding me that in the uncertainty, doubt, and fears,*
*You are an ever-present Friend and Savior. In Jesus' name, amen.*

# TRUE GREATNESS

*Who, being in very nature God, did not consider equality
with God something to be used to His own advantage;
rather, He made Himself nothing by taking the very nature
of a servant, being made in human likeness. And being found
in appearance as a man, He humbled Himself
by becoming obedient to death—even death on a cross!*

**PHILIPPIANS 2:6–8 NIV**

We humans often misunderstand humility. Some of us may think that acting in humility will reveal a weakness or make us vulnerable when we want to appear strong. We want to be respected and feared. We want people to depend on us and trust us, and sometimes we think that means we need to prove ourselves by not depending on anyone else but ourselves.

But true humility requires us to let go of pride and depend on God—not ourselves—for all that we need. And depending on God for strength and guidance and wisdom also involves obeying Him, even when it means letting go of something we've been holding on to.

Jesus provides the ultimate example of humility. "He humbled Himself by becoming obedient to death—even death on a cross!" He willingly relinquished His place in heaven to come to earth as a man so He could take the punishment for our sins and become a worthy sacrifice for us by dying on the cross.

Jesus humbled Himself, not by becoming weak, but by obedience. He learned obedience through suffering (Hebrews 5:8). And He invites to follow His example by obeying the Father, letting go of pride, and learning to depend fully on Him for everything that we need.

If you are struggling with a tendency to want to rely on yourself to meet all your needs, look to Jesus. Give Him your desire for self-sufficiency and ask Him to show you how to trust Him for everything in your life. And then watch how He takes your humble heart and grows you into a man of true greatness.

### PRAYER:

*We want to be great, Father, as You define greatness, so we ask You to teach us to depend on You and become more like Christ. In Jesus' name, amen.*

# INVISIBLE ENEMIES

*For we do not wrestle against flesh and blood,*
*but against the rulers, against the authorities,*
*against the cosmic powers over this present darkness,*
*against the spiritual forces of evil in the heavenly places.*

EPHESIANS 6:12 ESV

If asked to describe what makes our lives difficult, we might see the face of someone in our thoughts: a neighbor, a pushy coworker, a spouse, a rebellious child. Or maybe we think of a circumstance: a destructive habit, an unwanted diagnosis, an impossible deadline. We all face battles in life that involve people or circumstances that disrupt our peace or hinder us from accomplishing our goals. And we often respond by fighting back.

Some of our fights are petty arguments with people we live with or work with. Others are physical battles we fight to maintain our health or to heal our bodies or to accomplish a task. But God says our true opponents aren't "flesh and blood"; they are invisible spiritual enemies.

In his letter to the Christians in Ephesus, Paul reminds

us of the spiritual world—unseen but no less real than the person who always seems to know which buttons to push to upset us. Paul says spiritual warfare requires spiritual weapons, such as the helmet of salvation and the sword of the Spirit, which is God's Word (Ephesians 6:17). These equip us to defend ourselves from the enemy while helping us to grow in our faith in God.

We need to wrestle well, to be tough and relentless. And rather than wasting our energy on petty arguments with fellow humans, we need to be sure we are on the mat with the real enemy of our soul: "the spiritual forces of evil." Thankfully, we never have to fight these battles on our own. First John 4:4 tells us, "Little children, you are from God and have overcome them, for he who is in you is greater than he who is in the world" (ESV).

With God on your side, you have victory over the forces of evil that are trying to knock you down. Jesus has defeated evil through His death and resurrection.

### PRAYER:

*God, thank You for the victory we have in our spiritual battles because of Jesus. Thank You for saving me. Help me to fight the right battles and remember that You are greater than any enemy of my soul. In Jesus' name, amen.*

Never forget that
God isn't bound by the
way we are. We see only
the present moment;
GOD SEES
EVERYTHING.
We see only part of what He
is doing; He sees it all.

— BILLY GRAHAM —

# LIKE CHRIST IN
# A SURPRISING WAY

*For we do not have a high priest who is unable to empathize
with our weaknesses, but we have one who has been tempted
in every way, just as we are—yet He did not sin.*

HEBREWS 4:15 NIV

How do we feel when we are tempted to do something wrong? If we love Jesus and genuinely want to follow Him and honor God with our thoughts and actions, we probably feel horrified that we'd even consider to choose to sin when we are tempted. And we feel even worse when we give in to those temptations.

Not one of us escapes even one day without being tempted in some way to sin. Even Jesus was tempted in every way that we are. But—and here is a very big *but*—He did not sin. Jesus never asked the Father to forgive Him for terrible thoughts or for caving to any temptation to sin. Never.

Here's what we need to remember: Being tempted to sin is not a sin. When we are tempted to sin—whether the temptation comes to us by a thought, a person, a situation, a desire, or an image—we always have the choice to say no to it.

So, what do we do when despicable thoughts assault our minds or desires for something sinful overwhelm us? We can remind ourselves that Jesus walked on this same earth we walk on and faced the same kinds of thoughts and desires that we face, but He never gave in to them, and we don't need to act on them either.

When you face temptation, pray. Ask God to help you to walk away from temptation like Jesus did. Thank Him for giving you victory over temptation. And thank Him for His forgiveness for all the times you've messed up.

### PRAYER:

*Lord Jesus, You understand the struggles I face every day as a human. You know what it's like to be tempted to sin, and yet You never gave in to temptation. Thank You for setting the perfect example for me. Thank You for dying in my place to take the punishment for my sin so I can be forgiven. In Jesus' name, amen.*

# NOT ONLY YOU

*No temptation has overtaken you except what is common
to mankind. And God is faithful; He will not let you be
tempted beyond what you can bear. But when you are tempted,
He will also provide a way out so that you can endure it.*

I CORINTHIANS 10:13 NIV

**W**e are often ashamed of the sins that tempt us. We imagine a giant movie screen on which our temptations are displayed, much to our horror, and we cringe at the thought of what everyone might know about us. In those moments, Satan attacks us and whispers his lies: "It's okay. Nobody cares. Everybody does it."

And if we give in to the temptation, Satan no longer whispers. He shouts his shaming words at us: "I can't believe you did that! I thought you were a Christian! No true believer would ever do that. God can never forgive that sin. Shame on you!" Often, we wilt under those accusations, believing his lying voice.

But look again at God's Word. The phrase "common to mankind" in I Corinthians 10:13 might startle us. But it should encourage us. We are not alone in our temptations. God's people—our fellow brothers and sisters in the family of God—all suffer similar attacks.

God doesn't shame us for being tempted. Instead, He faithfully stands by His promise to us: "I will not let you be tempted too much or more than you can bear." He even says He will provide a way out. We are never forced to give in to temptation. God gives us the option of turning away from sin and trusting in His faithfulness to get us through difficult times. He also doesn't leave us on our own to endure temptation. He is with us, and He gives us other people who are also struggling with temptation and can offer us comfort and counsel.

These words remind us that God knows about our tough times and empathizes with us. He seals this promise with a profound statement about Himself: "And God is faithful." He is faithful even in the face of our temptations. He can be trusted—completely.

You are not alone in the struggle of temptation. God gives you other people, and most importantly, He gives you Himself.

## PRAYER:

*Thank You, Father, that I am not alone in the darker places of my life. Give me the faith to cling to You and to allow other believers to come alongside me in the struggles of life. In Jesus' name, amen.*

# FORGIVENESS
# AND JOY

*For I acknowledge my transgressions,*
*and my sin is always before me. Against You, You only,*
*have I sinned, and done this evil in Your sight.*

PSALM 51:3–4 NKJV

What could David have been thinking when he prayed this confession?

David had committed adultery with a woman named Bathsheba and then arranged for her husband, a man named Uriah, to be killed. The baby conceived from this adulterous affair died soon after birth. Then God sent the prophet Nathan to confront David with his terrible sin, and David repented.

Psalm 51 is David's prayer of confession. First, he acknowledges his sin. Then he acknowledges that he sinned against God. In verse 10 David asks God to create a "clean heart" within him and then says, "Restore to me the joy of Your salvation" (verse 12 NKJV).

David's confession and repentance did not change the earthly consequences of his actions—Uriah was still dead; David and Bathsheba's baby was still dead. But David's heart was changed. He wanted to get right with God. He wanted to experience the joy that can only come from a restored relationship with God.

This psalm of confession and repentance gives us evidence of why elsewhere in the Bible God calls David "a man after His own heart" (I Samuel 13:14; see Acts 13:22). Faced with the horrifying reality of his sin and its consequences, David understood that he had disobeyed God and that his relationship with God was in need of healing. He knew in his heart that what he needed most was God's forgiveness and mercy.

Not all of us commit adultery and murder like David did, but we all sin. And our sin keeps us from growing in our relationship with God. Is there sin in your life that you haven't repented of? Is it holding you back from having a relationship with God? Is it keeping you from experiencing joy? Ask God to help you follow in David's footsteps, and then confess your sin, repent of it—choose to turn from your sin and live in a way that honors God—and ask for God's forgiveness and mercy. And then go forward in the joy of His salvation.

### PRAYER:

*Father, forgive me for sinning against You. Help me to become more like David—more devoted to You than to anything or anyone else. In Jesus' name, amen.*

# ONE WAY TO FIX IT

*If we confess our sins, he is faithful and just to forgive us*
*our sins and to cleanse us from all unrighteousness.*

I JOHN 1:9 ESV

**W**e often like to try to fix things around the house ourselves. Sometimes we succeed; other times we make the situation worse and have to humbly admit we need help. And sometimes we take a similar approach to sin in our lives. We try to fix it. We try to do better. We try to put a bandage on the pain and keep going. Or we try to hide the mess in a closet and pretend it's not there. But sooner or later we have to admit we are miserable and that there's absolutely nothing we can do to fix it or clean it up.

Sometimes we are so miserable because of our sin and ashamed at the mess it's created in our lives that we just don't see a way out. Have you found yourself in this downward spiral of shame and misery? Maybe you've felt like you can never overcome a destructive habit. Maybe you don't feel worthy of God's forgiveness because of the weight of your guilt. Most of us have been there. But don't despair! There's hope.

In His Word, God promises to "forgive us our sins and to cleanse us from all unrighteousness" if we will admit our wrongdoing, ask for forgiveness, and trust that the death of Jesus—God's Son—on the cross is the only way to "fix" the problem of sin in our lives. When Jesus died on the cross, He took the punishment that we deserved. His sacrifice made it possible for God to forgive us and call us His children.

When we focus on ourselves rather than on God's promises and His faithfulness to us, it's easy to feel helpless and hopeless and completely miserable in our sin. But when we turn our focus to the One who promises to forgive us, we can accept His forgiveness and then start the process of allowing Him to clean up our lives.

Forgiveness is what we all need—not a bandage or a closet or a temporary solution. What will you confess to God today?

### PRAYER:

*Father, I easily forget Your promises.*
*Thank You that You remain faithful even when I do not.*
*In Jesus' name, amen.*

# THE SECRET GIFT

*I have learned to be content in whatever circumstances
I am.... I have learned the secret of being filled and going
hungry, both of having abundance and suffering need.
I can do all things through Him who strengthens me.*

PHILIPPIANS 4:11-13 NASB

Imagine the biggest, brightest Christmas tree, decked out with beautiful lights and precious ornaments that have been passed down from generation to generation. Wrapped, ribboned, and tagged presents—tempting everyone to sneak a peek—sit underneath the tree. But a priceless gift for the whole family is yet to be placed under the branches. This gift can't be wrapped—it has to be learned and taught.

This secret gift is contentment. The apostle Paul wrote to Christians in the first century AD about how he had learned to "be content in whatever circumstances" he was in— whether he was living with little resources or in a season of prosperity. He didn't live his life wanting more or demanding his circumstances to change. Instead, he had learned to be content knowing that God would provide for him and give him the strength to face anything in his life.

The priceless gift of contentment is just as needed and relevant today as it was two thousand years ago. As men, we can give this gift to our families and loved ones by learning it ourselves and then modeling it, so they, too, can discover the secret of being content. We can learn to let go of the pressures of working harder and harder to get more and more and instead find time to enjoy what we already have with the people who matter most.

In learning contentment—rather than fixating on accumulating things or changing our circumstances—our families will be more satisfied and peaceful than ever before. This priceless gift is one we'll never find under any tree, and it's one that will never need to be exchanged or returned to the store.

In a digital world where advertisements constantly bombard us by telling us we need more—often leading us to max our credit cards to get whatever our hearts desire—God reminds us to be content with what we have and to rely on His strength for all that He has for us to accomplish.

PRAYER:

*Father, help me to learn the secret of being content.*
*In Jesus' name, amen.*

# SETTING UP THE GOALPOSTS

*Now this is eternal life: that they know You,*
*the only true God, and Jesus Christ, whom You have sent.*

JOHN 17:3 NIV

Goalposts keep watch over high school football fields, and Friday nights are filled with excitement during football season.

The Christian life is another field, but one of blood, sweat, and tears. Yet, at the end stands a goalpost of eternal value—eternal life. Many of us refer to this eternal life as a place called heaven. We dream of this place where pain, guilt, and tears are absent and where we will never again struggle with sin or disappointment or temptation.

We are comforted with that dream and long to escape this painful life. But what if we have set up the goalposts short of the end zone? What if there is more and better for us? Suppose we could have eternal life *now*, starting before death?

In Jesus' prayer in John 17:3, offered only hours before His crucifixion, He encourages us with some great news. He gives us the true definition of eternal life. He says it involves not going somewhere or doing something, but knowing *Someone*.

Eternal life is more than a safe place to retire. Eternal life is knowing God through Jesus. It is living in the presence of God. This intimacy with God begins when we give our hearts to Him. Eternal life has already begun for those who know God personally.

We are already in the end zone doing our touchdown celebration dance. This relationship with God grows with each day of knowing Jesus. We no longer fear death. Death has no sting. Joy comes each morning—here, on earth!

Are you living in the joy of knowing God through Jesus now? Are you making the most of every opportunity each day to spend time with your Creator and thank Him for His gift of eternal life? If not, what is holding you back?

### PRAYER:

*What a gift from You, Lord, that we can know You and enjoy this life with You. Thank You for eternal life, Father. In Jesus' name, amen.*

# CASTING
# YOUR CARES

*Humble yourselves, therefore, under the mighty hand of God,*
*so that He may exalt you at the proper time,*
*casting all your cares on Him, because He cares about you.*

I PETER 5:6–7 CSB

I n these verses from I Peter, the word *casting* isn't about trout fishing or how to tie and cast a fly. We'll leave that for guys who know how to do it. Rather, it's about the mess we get into when our stubborn pride keeps us from asking for help.

Peter's words about "casting" our cares on God come right after Peter's instruction about humility. Isn't it great that God would entrust these inspired words to Peter, the disciple who was so proud that he once announced to Jesus that he would never deny Him—even if everyone else did—but then proceeded to deny Jesus not once, but *three times*?

Peter wrote these words after he had received Jesus' forgiveness. He'd clearly learned a lesson in humility and wanted to share that lesson with his readers.

We are often bound by the cares and worries of this world. We imagine we can fix everything by just trying harder, but it is never that simple. Sometimes, the harder we try, the more frustrated we become, and we end up throwing our hands in the air and giving up.

Peter tells us to cast our cares on God, the One who created us and knows every detail about us and about our lives. The reason we are often reluctant to give Him everything we are concerned or anxious about is because we pridefully figure we can roll up our sleeves and do it ourselves, which never turns out well.

Casting our cares on God is not a sign of weakness. Doing so reveals a humble spirit—a man who is willing to let go of pride and admit his need for God.

### PRAYER:

*Father, You know me and my prideful tendencies. Forgive me for that pride and teach me to cast all my cares on You. In Jesus' name, amen.*

# THE ULTIMATE GOAL

*But the goal of our instruction is love from a pure heart,*
*from a good conscience, and from a sincere faith.*

I TIMOTHY 1:5 NASB

If we want the right goal for our lives and the right goal for teaching our children or setting an example for younger people in our lives, we've come to the right verse.

Paul writes to Timothy, his young protégé in the faith, and tells him the ultimate goal in spreading the message of Jesus is to love well. It would be pointless to teach someone about Jesus if we have no love for that person. Would people see Jesus more clearly if we merely recite parts of the Bible to them? Hopefully. But the surest way for people to see Jesus is in the way we love them while we tell them about the truths in God's Word. Imagine if love were the goal in our families and in our churches!

Love comes from a pure heart, a good conscience, and a sincere faith. A pure heart implies we have a heart like the Lord Jesus. We begin not with how much we know, but with a grateful attitude. We let others know how our lives have been forever changed because of the forgiveness we have received through Christ—not because of anything we've done or haven't done. Our hearts are filtered daily by our repentance and pursuit of God.

Our love also comes from a good conscience—a conscience that is honest and can discern good from evil. A conscience that understands that God's grace is something that others need to know about. We can't keep that kind of good news to ourselves and have a clear conscience.

Finally, love flows from sincere faith. The sincerity of our faith is measured not so much in size as in direction. Our faith is only as sincere as the object of our faith. God is pure, true, and worthy of our trust. Any faith placed in Him is sincere.

Love others, and teach the people in your life who look up to you to love well too. Love from a pure heart, a good conscience, and a sincere faith.

### PRAYER:

*God, help me to love well. Teach me to love You first before all else. In Jesus' name, amen.*

# INTENTIONAL
# AND POWERFUL

*One day Jesus was teaching, and Pharisees and teachers of the law were sitting there. They had come from every village of Galilee and from Judea and Jerusalem. And the power of the Lord was with Jesus to heal the sick.*

LUKE 5:17 NIV

What words do you use to describe Jesus? Maybe words like *compassionate*, *loving*, *unselfish*, *kind*, *forgiving*, and *merciful* come to mind. What about *powerful*? Luke tells us that "the power of the Lord was with Jesus to heal the sick." Wherever Jesus went while He was on this earth, He took the power of God with Him. And He used that power to miraculously change people's lives. And yet He was selective in how He used that power. He didn't use it to work mighty miracles every second of every day. He used it in intentional ways to show His deep love for people and to help them understand His identity as the Son of God.

In Luke 5:17–26 we read how Jesus healed a paralyzed man. Jesus powerfully worked in this man's life in a public setting—where religious leaders who opposed Jesus stood watching. Jesus could have chosen any place to heal this man, but He wanted to show His audience that the Son of God was in their presence. Even so, some people who witnessed this amazing miracle still refused to put their faith in Him.

Do you ever doubt God's ability and desire to work in your life? What changes in your current circumstances are you waiting for? What needs do you have that haven't been met yet? Are you trusting God to work out those changes and meet those needs?

God is still powerfully working on the earth today, even if we don't understand His actions or His timing. He is intentional with His love and care for us. Will you trust Him with each step you take and have faith that He will be with you and sustain you in all that you're going through right now?

## PRAYER:

*Father, thank You for Jesus, who came to this earth to show Your love for the people You created. Thank You for Your power. Help me to trust that You will work in my life in Your ways and in Your timing. In Jesus' name, amen.*

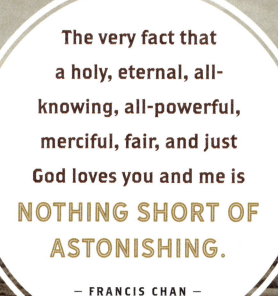

The very fact that
a holy, eternal, all-
knowing, all-powerful,
merciful, fair, and just
God loves you and me is

NOTHING SHORT OF
ASTONISHING.

— FRANCIS CHAN —

# WHOM DO
# YOU LOVE?

*Jesus said to him, "You shall love the LORD your God*
*with all your heart, with all your soul, and with all your mind."*
MATTHEW 22:37 NKJV

**M**any of us fixate on being liked, even loved, by other people. We have become a generation of people-pleasers, looking for every opportunity to impress others, win the favor of others, or get them to vote for us. Advertisers seize on this, promising that if we use their product, people will like us. We believe the lie that we need to elevate ourselves in order to have worth or significance. We have imagined a different great commandment than the one Jesus issued.

Jesus commanded us to love God with all that is within us. This contradicts the "command" that our culture wants us to follow: "Thou shalt be loved." When we are deceived into believing we should love ourselves above anything or anyone else, we work with all the strength and cleverness we can muster to prioritize our own feelings, our own goals, our own agendas, even our own rights. But following this deceptive command only leads to our ruin.

When we focus our love on ourselves rather than on God and other people, our relationships with God and others suffer. We miss out on experiencing all that a relationship with God can bring us—things like joy, peace, contentment, safety, and hope. Living to serve and honor ourselves will never satisfy us.

What motivates you to get up in the morning? What is your focus at work, at home, at church? Whom are you ultimately living for, loving, and serving? Whom do you love the most? If you've been keeping yourself and your own interests at the top of your priority list, consider how putting God as number one will change your life.

### PRAYER:

*Lord, help me to let go of my desire to love myself more than I love You. Help me to learn how to love, serve, and honor You with all that I do, say, and think. Thank You for patiently teaching me what really matters in this life. In Jesus' name, amen.*

# THE BEST QUESTION

*This is what the L\ord says:*
*"What did your ancestors find wrong with Me that led them*
*to stray so far from Me? They worshiped worthless idols,*
*only to become worthless themselves. They did not ask,*
*'Where is the L\ord who brought us safely out of Egypt?'"*

JEREMIAH 2:5–6 NLT

God spoke to the prophet Jeremiah and told him to speak His message to the people of Judah, who had abandoned Him.

God accused the people of Judah of forgetting about Him and all that He had done for them in rescuing them out of slavery in Egypt and bringing them to the Promised Land. The people had turned to idols and neglected to seek God. They stopped asking, "Where is the L\ord?" Even the priests, the religious leaders of Judah, were not seeking God. Because of their refusal to turn back to God, the people were taken into captivity by their enemies, the Babylonians.

So often we find ourselves in difficult circumstances in life, and we ask ourselves all kinds of questions: Do I have enough money? What will my friends think? Can I live without this right now? How will I tell my family? How will I make it through today?

How long does it take us before we ask the *best* question: "Where are You, Lord?" Why do we try to solve our problems without Him? What will it take for us to remember all that He has done in our lives, acknowledge Him, and learn to seek Him? We forget His presence with us. We forget His infinite love for us. We forget His promises. Yet He wants us to look to Him and to ask for His help. He wants to be a part of every decision we make.

Will you let Him? Will you trust Him and depend on Him to work in your life for your good?

### PRAYER:

*Lord, forgive me for ignoring You when I should be seeking You. I don't want to make any decision without asking You about it. I trust You and Your plan for my life. In Jesus' name, amen.*

# GODLINESS
# REDEFINED

*Therefore let everyone who is godly offer prayer
to you at a time when you may be found.*

PSALM 32:6 ESV

Here is amazingly good news, if only we will pay attention. In Psalm 32, David describes what it's like to be utterly consumed by unforgiven sin: "When I kept silent, my bones wasted away through my groaning all day long" (verse 3 ESV). But after David confesses his sin to God, he prays, "I acknowledged my sin to you, and I did not cover my iniquity; I said, 'I will confess my transgressions to the LORD,' and you forgave the iniquity of my sin" (verse 5 ESV).

What man doesn't need to read this psalm of repentance? Don't we nod our heads in agreement when David speaks of his body wasting away and of his groaning all day long when he failed to repent? We've all messed up badly. We've all felt this level of shame and pain because of our sin. Maybe we lied or boasted, and the guilt ate us up inside until we confessed and repented. But then we found relief because of God's forgiveness. We can say, along with David, "Blessed is the one whose transgression is forgiven, whose sin is covered" (verse 1 ESV).

God redefines *godliness* in this psalm. Verse 6 begins with "therefore," which connects what came before with what follows. What came before is honest, painful grieving over real sin, followed by heartfelt confession. But listen to what follows: "Let everyone who is godly offer prayer." God tells us that godliness doesn't involve perfection. Rather, godliness is a result of honest confession and repentance. Hope comes with this good news.

If you sincerely desire to be a godly man, know that God has placed that longing inside you. Your job is to pray—keep the line of communication between you and God open. Pray fervently, with a heart that repents of sin and seeks to honor and follow Jesus. This is what godliness is all about.

### PRAYER:

*Thank You, Father, for hope because You do forgive me. Thank You for making me godly. In Jesus' name, amen.*

# SEEKING GOD

*How can a young man keep his way pure? By keeping it*
*according to Your word. With all my heart I have sought You;*
*do not let me wander from Your commandments.*
*I have treasured Your word in my heart,*
*so that I may not sin against You.*

**PSALM 119:9–11 NASB**

The words of the psalmist in these verses reveal his desire
to honor God with his thoughts and actions. They also
reveal that the temptation to give in to impure thoughts
and actions is a temptation that is common to all men—
throughout all decades and centuries and millennia of human
history.

The psalmist asks the question, "How can a young man
keep his way pure?" And then he immediately answers the
question: "By keeping it according to Your word." Seems pretty
simple. If we follow God's Word and obey His commands,
surely we can gain victory over impure thoughts and actions.
And treasuring God's Word—by learning and memorizing
Scripture—will certainly help us not to sin against our Creator.

But there's another important truth within these verses in Psalm 119. In between the parts about staying pure by keeping God's Word and treasuring His Word in our hearts is this often-overlooked statement: "With all my heart I have sought You." The psalmist realized that what he desperately needed was to seek after and to know God. Without God, he would never be able to run from temptation to sin. Without God, nothing else mattered.

We don't come to God's Word merely to be fixed. We come to His Word to find Him, to know Him, to *be with Him*. We want victory over temptation in our lives, and this requires seeking God and depending on Him for the strength and endurance to fight our battles against anger and lust and pride.

We can memorize all the right verses and try to obey all the rules. But those things won't matter if we neglect our relationship with God. When we do those things while seeking God through prayer, loving Him, and desiring to know Him more each day, we stay focused on Him and have a stronger motivation for wanting to remain pure.

### PRAYER:

*O God, how I need You. Turn me away from thoughts about myself and lead me closer to You. In Jesus' name, amen.*

# SET A GUARD
# OVER MY MOUTH

*Set a guard over my mouth, Lᴏʀᴅ;*
*keep watch over the door of my lips.*

PSALM 141:3 NIV

We need a full-time guard over our mouths. We can get into so much trouble so quickly with the words we use to communicate.

James tells us our mouths are like small sparks that are capable of setting entire forests ablaze (James 3:5). We could fill up many books and cause a lot of pain if the careless words we have spoken were exposed for all to see. In our online world, how many stories are told of marriages shattered or jobs lost or reputations ruined because of careless texts, posts, or emails?

How can we take better care of our words, whether spoken or written? David asked God to set a guard over his mouth, and then he prayed, "Do not let my heart be drawn to what is evil" (Psalm 141:4 niv). Our hearts are connected to our mouths. What we are filling our eyes and minds and hearts with ultimately comes out of our mouths. Jesus said, "The mouth speaks what the heart is full of" (Matthew 12:34 niv). If our hearts lean toward evil, our mouths will follow.

With what are you filling your heart? What steps have you taken to filter what goes into your heart through your eyes and ears? If you're struggling with this and need divine intervention to help you filter out the evil you are allowing into your heart, you can pray the same prayer that David prayed by asking God to set a guard over your mouth and to keep your heart from being drawn to what is evil.

Seek the Lord with all your heart. If your heart is filled with all that is good and decent, your tongue—and your written communication—will follow.

### PRAYER:

*Father, I need a guard set over my mouth. I don't want to say or write anything that would dishonor You or bring shame upon other people or upon myself. Please help me to seek after what is good and not be drawn to evil. In Jesus' name, amen.*

# A NEW REPUTATION

*I have been crucified with Christ;*
*and it is no longer I who live, but Christ lives in me;*
*and the life which I now live in the flesh I live by faith*
*in the Son of God, who loved me and gave Himself up for me.*

**GALATIANS 2:20 NASB**

These words are a stark contrast to the me-first mentality. Paul the apostle, once guilty of capturing Christians and having them killed for believing in Jesus, wrote in Galatians that he had "been crucified with Christ." His words "It is no longer I" could stand alone as a testimony to his changed life.

Paul could have felt stuck in shame because of his reputation as a persecutor of Christians. He could have avoided situations where he would be confronted by the families and friends of the people he had previously harmed. He could have chosen to hide his faith and instead live his life in a way that detracted attention from himself. He could have put himself first and lived only for the sake of Paul.

Instead, Paul obediently followed Jesus and dedicated his life to preaching the gospel everywhere he went—even if people doubted his sincerity, his motives, or his integrity. He knew his purpose for living was no longer rooted in himself; he lived solely for Christ. His response to Jesus' death on the cross should be our response—full surrender to living for Jesus.

Do you feel trapped in a reputation that you earned in the past? Do you feel you need to hide from it or work to rid yourself of it? Are you willing to let go of what others think of you and instead embrace the changes God has made in your life because of your faith in Jesus?

If you are a child of God, you get to trade in your old reputation for a new one. Your new reputation should reflect a heart that is surrendered to Jesus and to His character. Are you ready to break free from putting yourself first and allow Christ to fully live in you?

### PRAYER:

*Father, please help me to be concerned more about my reputation as Your child than about my reputation as anything else. Help me to live for You in the roles You have given me. I want Your reputation to be all that matters and all that people see when they look at my life. In Jesus' name, amen.*

# A GRACIOUS GOD

*I knew that You are a gracious and compassionate God,*
*slow to anger, abounding in faithful love,*
*and one who relents from sending disaster.*

JONAH 4:2 CSB

Suppose God's voice awakened you from a sound sleep and you heard Him tell you to get up and travel across the county to tell your archenemy—the *one* who betrayed you and hurt you—about God's grace and forgiveness. Would you jump out of bed, make your travel arrangements, and head for this person's home? Or would you tell God there's no way you would *ever* face this person—let alone offer them forgiveness—and then bury your head under your pillow?

The prophet Jonah faced a similar choice—but on a much bigger scale. When God told Jonah to travel to the city of Nineveh to tell the people to repent of their wicked ways or face punishment from God, Jonah refused to go at first. He knew God's character, that God is "a gracious and compassionate God . . . who relents from sending disaster." Jonah knew if the people of Nineveh repented of their sin,

God would not destroy them. Jonah hated the inhabitants of Jonah—they were Assyrians and enemies of God's people, the Israelites. But God gives every person—regardless of what they look like, where they live, or what they've done—the same chance to receive His grace and forgiveness. The Ninevites were no exception.

Jonah ended up going to Nineveh, although reluctantly. And after the people of Nineveh repented, Jonah sat and sulked—angry with God for saving the people of a nation at war with Israel.

Jonah's story could have ended differently. He could have celebrated God's grace and His faithfulness to the people of Nineveh. Instead, he wallowed in anger and self-pity. His unforgiving heart brought him nothing but misery.

When God asks you to show kindness, love, or forgiveness to someone who has angered you, abused you, or betrayed you, how do you respond? God will give you the strength to forgive others, and when you do, peace—instead of misery—will fill your heart.

### PRAYER:

*Lord, it's difficult to forgive sometimes.*
*Please reveal to me the people I need to forgive,*
*and fill my life with Your peace. In Jesus' name, amen.*

# BE A DOER

*But be doers of the word,*
*and not hearers only, deceiving yourselves.*
**JAMES 1:22 NKJV**

Reading or hearing God's Word is not the same thing as *doing* what God tells us to do in the Bible. This may seem obvious, but we humans often need to be reminded of seemingly obvious things as we actively and willingly apply the truth to our lives.

The Bible is not just filled with interesting stories and teachings; it's the means by which God has chosen to communicate to His people and to help us know Him. He wants us to read His Word—to hear it and study it and spend time learning it. But our interaction with God's Word also involves living out God's truths and teachings and commandments.

Second Timothy 3:16–17 tells us that "all Scripture is given by inspiration of God, and is profitable for doctrine, for reproof, for correction, for instruction in righteousness, that the man of God may be complete, thoroughly equipped for every good work" (NKJV). God Himself speaks through the chapters and verses of the Bible and invites us be changed, to be complete, to be equipped to live as men of God.

We come to God's Word, not as a mere exercise or spiritual discipline, but *in a relationship*. We listen to God's voice in the words we read. We respond by doing what He has called us to do. We learn how to live as His children, and then we apply what we learn to our lives each day.

Jesus told His disciples, "When the Father sends the Advocate as My representative—that is, the Holy Spirit—He will teach you everything and will remind you of everything I have told you" (John 14:26 NLT). You're not on your own when it comes to doing God's Word. The Holy Spirit will help you to learn and reflect on God's Word, and He will remind you of what you've learned when you are putting it into practice in real time.

### PRAYER:

*What an honor that You would let me know You, God. Thank You for Your Word and for Your Spirit, who helps me put Your Word into practice. I want to be a man of God who is a doer of Your Word. In Jesus' name, amen.*

# TWO SINS

*For My people have committed two sins: they have turned away from Me, the spring of fresh water, and they have dug cisterns, cracked cisterns that can hold no water at all.*

JEREMIAH 2:13 GNT

What? Two sins? Only two?

The nation of Judah surely committed more than two sins. But God explains two to the prophet Jeremiah. First, they had "turned away from" Him, "the spring of fresh water." Second, they had dug for themselves "cracked cisterns that can hold no water."

The first sin involved rejecting God. When people are introduced to God, they have a choice: accept Him or reject Him. The second sin involved trying to find their way and make their own plans without involving God.

This pattern is the way all of us turn our backs on God. We first say no to Him and then yes to ourselves. We do this when we choose to ignore God's ways and instead try to succeed at something in life on our own. This leaves us empty, like a cracked cistern that holds no water.

Notice the order of the sins in this verse in Jeremiah. First the people turn away from God; then they are unsuccessful in digging a functional cistern. If we turn to God in obedience and love, He will provide all we need from His spring of fresh water that never runs dry. We won't even need to dig our own cisterns—He provides our lives with meaning and value and fulfillment. But when we neglect our relationship with God, looking to find fulfillment and meaning and value in the things we do ourselves, nothing we do will ever fill us with those things.

Are you depending on God as your source of fresh water—your source for meaning, value, and fulfillment? Or are you digging cracked cisterns—trying to find meaning in things that will never satisfy you?

### PRAYER:

*Lord, help me to turn to You and not away from You.*
*Forgive me for trying to find meaning apart from You.*
*Thank You for being the Source of all I need.*
*In Jesus' name, amen.*

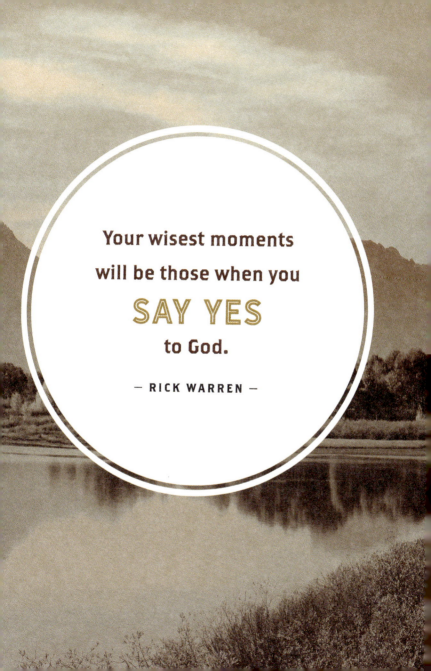

Your wisest moments
will be those when you
SAY YES
to God.

— RICK WARREN —

# HONORING AND UNDERSTANDING

*In the same way, you husbands must give honor to your wives.*
*Treat your wife with understanding as you live together....*
*Treat her as you should so your prayers will not be hindered.*

### I PETER 3:7 NLT

**F**or men who are married or in a relationship, this is where warning signs shoot up everywhere: "Caution. Deep and Snaky Waters." How often do we throw up our hands in surrender and cry, "I don't understand this person!"?

God no doubt understands our dilemma—after all, He created men and women—but He doesn't accept our excuses for mistreating people. He warns us that when we neglect to honor our loved ones or treat them with understanding, our prayers to Him will be "hindered." God clearly cares about how we treat the people we claim to love!

How often does it seem like your prayers bounce back to you off the ceiling? Have you ever considered that the way you are treating another person—your wife, if you are married, or another loved one—could be part of the reason? Have you struggled to pray while also neglecting to treat those you love in an understanding way? The apostle Peter says there's a connection.

God designed people to think and act in unique ways, and our job is to learn how the people God has placed in our lives are uniquely designed so we can better honor and understand them.

Don't be foolish and pretend that other people were designed in the same way you were. Take the time to listen to the people you love, to find out what their weaknesses and strengths are, to get to know the people God uniquely designed them to be. If you're married or in a relationship, your significant other may be smarter than you, and she's likely more attractive, but you have been commanded to honor her and to understand her. Be careful, listen well, and pray a lot.

### PRAYER:

*O Lord, help me to better honor and understand the people You have placed in my life. Thank You for Your strength and courage in my relationships. In Jesus' name, amen.*

# GOD'S PURPOSE
# FOR YOUR LIFE

*And we know that God causes all things
to work together for good to those who love God,
to those who are called according to His purpose.*

ROMANS 8:28 NASB

The question that begs for an answer is "What is God's purpose?"

The next verse answers that question: "For those whom He foreknew, He also predestined to become conformed to the image of His Son" (Romans 8:29 NASB). God's purpose for those who love Him and have been called by Him is for us to become more like Jesus.

God typically uses two things to make us more like Jesus: God's Word and suffering. We learn about Jesus' character and His compassionate actions when we read and study the Bible. God changes our hearts to become more like Jesus when we learn to love like Him, forgive like Him, pray like Him, and obey like Him. But part of Jesus' obedience to His Father involved suffering. The writer of Hebrews tells us, "Although He [Jesus] was a Son, He learned obedience from the things which He suffered" (5:8 NASB).

How many times have we cried out to God to give us a break and take away the hard stuff from our lives? If we listen carefully, we might hear Him say, "Make up your mind. Do you want to be like Jesus, or do you want Me to take away your suffering?" And if we're being honest, our answer is often for our suffering to be eased.

If we want to be like Jesus, we'll need to be willing to suffer for His sake. Our struggles—our physical ailments, our challenging relationships with coworkers or family members, our financial woes, our addictions and bad habits—give us plenty of opportunities to obediently follow Jesus' lead in how we pray and interact with others. In our suffering, we can choose to obey God or reject Him. When we obey Him, our faith is strengthened, and we become more and more conformed to the image of Jesus.

Will you submit to God's purpose and plan so that you can be more like Jesus?

### PRAYER:

*Lord, I do want to be like You. Although suffering stinks, I can't imagine that I could learn obedience without it. Make me fearless and strong in the face of suffering. In Jesus' name, amen.*

# WHAT BELONGS TO GOD?

*"Tell us then, what is Your opinion? Is it right to pay the imperial tax to Caesar or not?" But Jesus, knowing their evil intent, said, "You hypocrites, why are you trying to trap Me? Show Me the coin used for paying the tax." They brought Him a denarius, and He asked them, "Whose image is this? And whose inscription?" "Caesar's," they replied. Then He said to them, "So give back to Caesar what is Caesar's, and to God what is God's." When they heard this, they were amazed. So they left Him and went away.*

MATTHEW 22:17–22 NIV

The Pharisees were trying to trap Jesus into saying something that would give them a reason to have Him arrested. They sent some people to ask Jesus whether it was right to pay taxes to the Roman government. If Jesus had answered no, they would have accused Him of rebelling against the Roman authorities. But their question didn't stump Jesus. He knew "their evil intent," and He gave them an answer they couldn't refute.

What belonged to Caesar had his image stamped on it. But what belongs to God? What is God's image "stamped" on? The answer is *us*. God designed men and women and made us in His image. Genesis 1:27 says, "God created mankind in His own image" (NIV). To be made in God's image means we can think, feel, and make choices as God does.

In the garden of Eden, Adam and Eve enjoyed a close relationship with God. But they lost that relationship when they gave in to temptation and sinned. God sent His Son, Jesus, to restore the relationship with God that was lost in the garden. By His mercy and grace, we learn to trust and love Jesus, and to let Him make us more like Him. The more we love Him and follow Him, the more of ourselves we give to Him.

What are you doing to give more of yourself to God? Are you growing in your relationship with Him? Are you giving your time, finances, and talents to serve people in need whom God also created in His image? What steps can you take to begin looking more like Jesus?

## PRAYER:

*Father, thank You for creating me in Your image.*
*I want to look more and more like You. Help me to focus my life*
*on giving to You what belongs to You. In Jesus' name, amen.*

# A HEALING
# AND A WARNING

*Immediately the man became well,*
*and picked up his pallet and began to walk.*

JOHN 5:9 NASB

Jesus healed a man who had been sick and unable to walk for thirty-eight years. What a wonderful picture of the kindness and power of Jesus.

The story of healing doesn't end with the man getting up and walking. Jesus later found the man at the temple and warned him, "Behold, you have become well; do not sin anymore, so that nothing worse happens to you" (John 5:14 NASB). The story ends with the healed man telling people "that it was Jesus who had made him well" (verse 15 NASB).

For years this man had provided for himself by begging. Then Jesus came along and gave him the chance to live a new life—both physically and spiritually. It was up to the healed man to choose how he would live. Jesus knew that the eternal consequence of living in sin is infinitely worse than living with a physical ailment.

We are given the same choice. We need to decide whether our spiritual health is more important than our physical health and then live accordingly. Jesus offers us His healing and compassion, but His greatest gift to us is Himself. And when we acknowledge that He has died to save us from the consequence of our sin and we trust Him as our Savior, we won't want to continue living in sin and shame. He has made us well!

When you cry out to God for healing—whether physical, spiritual, or emotional—remember what is *most* important. And like the man who was able to walk after thirty-eight years, don't keep the identity of your Healer to yourself. Spread the news of Jesus so others can experience the eternal healing of their souls.

### PRAYER:

*God, thank You for Your compassion. Thank You that I can come to You and ask for healing. Help me to choose to live for You each day and to turn far away from sinful thoughts and actions. Thank You for Your grace. In Jesus' name, amen.*

# A SHIFT

*How long, Lord? Will You forget me forever?*
*How long will You hide Your face from me?*
*How long must I wrestle with my thoughts and day after day*
*have sorrow in my heart? How long will my enemy triumph*
*over me? Look on me and answer, Lord my God. Give light to*
*my eyes, or I will sleep in death, and my enemy will say, "I have*
*overcome him," and my foes will rejoice when I fall. But I trust*
*in Your unfailing love; my heart rejoices in Your salvation.*
*I will sing the Lord's praise, for He has been good to me.*

PSALM 13:1–6 NIV

**H**ow honest should we dare to be with God?

This prayer of David is the benchmark of how to trust God in tough times. David wants to know if God will forget him forever, if God will continue hiding His face from him, and how long he must continue wrestling with his thoughts while sorrow infiltrates his heart. We might imagine lightning falling from heaven at the sound of such a prayer.

But then there is a shift in the prayer. David's words—and his focus—suddenly change. David moves from his sorrow to saying, "But I trust in Your unfailing love." This is the same David who moments ago had accused God of forgetting him and hiding from him.

David trusted God so deeply that he was comfortable voicing his pain in the presence of God without fear of reprisal. Where did that trust come from? David trusted in God for salvation and sang the Lord's praise because God had been good to him. David may have been experiencing a period of great suffering in his life, but when he focused on God's love and His goodness, he could rejoice and sing. That's what trusting in God can do for us too.

In the middle of your pain, lift your eyes up to the One whose unfailing love, salvation, and goodness are trustworthy. When you do, it will change your grieving into rejoicing.

### PRAYER:

*Lord, thank You for letting me speak to You honestly. I don't want to hold anything back from You. But most of all, thank You that I can trust You and that Your love and goodness never leave me. In Jesus' name, amen.*

# A MAN AFTER GOD'S HEART

*After removing Saul, He made David their king.*
*God testified concerning him: "I have found David*
*son of Jesse, a man after My own heart;*
*he will do everything I want him to do."*

ACTS 13:22 NIV

How would you describe a "man after God's own heart"? Does your life resemble any part of that description? King David of Israel probably never considered himself such a man—which made him even more that kind of man.

God regards obedience as the defining quality of a man after His heart. This man will do everything God wants him to do. David certainly did not do everything God wanted. He committed adultery and arranged a murder! So how did he qualify as a man after God's heart?

In Psalm 32, written by David, God redefines godliness not as perfection, but as grieving and repenting when we sin. A man who wants to be a godly man, who grieves over his sin and turns to God in repentance, does so only if God puts that desire in his heart. We should be thankful when God places this desire in our hearts. Paul reminds us in his letter to the Philippians that when God begins a good work in us, He will bring it to completion (1:6). He doesn't abandon us when we mess up. He doesn't tell us we're out of chances for forgiveness. He continues His good work in our hearts.

David was not perfect, but he repented deeply for his sins. One of the most important virtues of a man after God's own heart is the desire to repent. God uses our repentant and humbled hearts to bring us closer to the image of His Son.

What will it take to make you a man after God's own heart?

### PRAYER:

*God, I want to be like Jesus. I want to obey You and to be called a man after Your own heart. Do whatever You please to make that true of me. In Jesus' name, amen.*

# STRONGER FAITH

*"Simon, Simon, Satan has asked to sift all of you as wheat.*
*But I have prayed for you, Simon, that your faith may not fail.*
*And when you have turned back, strengthen your brothers."*

LUKE 22:31–32 NIV

Jesus prayed specific, personal prayers for His followers. During Jesus' last supper with His disciples before His crucifixion, He prayed that Peter's faith would not fail. He knew that Peter's faith would soon falter—Peter would deny knowing Jesus not once but three times. We would consider Peter's denial of Jesus an epic failure of faith.

But Jesus knew Peter's faith would ultimately be strengthened and that Peter would turn back to Him. And so Jesus also prayed that when Peter "turned back," he would "strengthen" other Christians in their faith.

Jesus understood that Peter's denial wasn't the end of his faith. Peter fell, but he didn't stay down. He "wept bitterly" over failing his Savior and Friend (Luke 22:62 NIV).

Peter learned from his experience of failure and moved forward in his faith. He didn't let his past failures hold him down. After Jesus ascended to heaven, Peter unashamedly preached the gospel and introduced many people to the Savior, Jesus. Because he had experienced failure, he could encourage others when they fell down. And because he had grown stronger in his faith, he could help others grow strong too.

We all let Jesus down from time to time. We all fall. And we all need our faith strengthened. God wants us to get back up, turn to Him, learn from our failures, and then encourage others in their journeys of faith.

Before His death, Jesus prayed this prayer: "My prayer is not for them [Jesus' disciples] alone. I pray also for those who will believe in Me through their message, that all of them may be one, Father, just as You are in Me and I am in You" (John 17:20–21 NIV).

If you are a follower of Jesus, know that Jesus prayed for you, just as He prayed for Peter. Leave your failures and mistakes in the past, where they belong. And take courage as you move forward in faith, knowing you belong to God.

### PRAYER:

*Lord, thank You for praying for Your followers.*
*Thank You for the encouragement in the life of Peter,*
*who didn't let his failures define him. In Jesus' name, amen.*

# A HOLY CALLING

*But like the Holy One who called you,*
*be holy yourselves also in all your behavior.*
*I Peter 1:15 NASB*

If God is holy, and holiness is the ultimate standard, how can the apostle Peter—who wrote the words in today's verse—possibly expect us even to come close to living holy lives? Peter certainly didn't live a sinless life, but Peter knew what it means to be forgiven, loved, and accepted by his Savior, Jesus. And because of his faith in Jesus, he could encourage people to "be holy" in all their thoughts and actions.

The apostle Paul helps us understand how we can live holy lives. He wrote that God "made Him [Jesus] who knew no sin to be sin on our behalf, so that we might become the righteousness of God in Him" (II Corinthians 5:21 NASB). The truth is that no one but Jesus has ever lived, or will ever live, a sinless life. But Jesus took our sin on Himself so that God will look on us as though we are without sin. We "become the righteousness of God" in Jesus. And that, my friends, is how we live holy lives. It's not us—it's Jesus *in us*.

Because of our faith in Jesus, we can come before a holy God with all our ugly failures and receive complete forgiveness. We can then choose to live each day doing our best to honor Him with our lives as a way of praising Him and loving Him and thanking Him for His grace and goodness to us. The more we understand what Jesus has done for us and who God created us to be, the more we'll want to look and act like our Savior.

The miracle is that we are men designed in the image of God. Our sin damages that image. But because Jesus has taken our sin upon Himself, we can live holy lives as forgiven sons of God.

### PRAYER:

*Thank You, Father, for Your grace and Your forgiveness.*
*You have called me to live a holy life.*
*Help me to live in a way that honors You in my thoughts*
*and actions. In Jesus' name, amen.*

# ASKING FOR A SIGN

*Then Gideon said to God, "If You are truly going to use me to rescue Israel as You promised, prove it to me in this way. I will put a wool fleece on the threshing floor tonight. If the fleece is wet with dew in the morning but the ground is dry, then I will know that You are going to help me rescue Israel as You promised." And that is just what happened. When Gideon got up early the next morning, he squeezed the fleece and wrung out a whole bowlful of water.*

**JUDGES 6:36–38 NLT**

Gideon wasn't a warrior or a leader of any kind. So when God told him that he would defeat the enemies of the people of Israel, Gideon had some serious questions. He asked God to prove that what He said would truly happen. And God graciously reassured Gideon—not once, but twice.

Zechariah, the father of John the Baptist, had a different outcome when he questioned God. When an angel from God told him that he would have a son, Zechariah couldn't believe it because he and his wife were too old to have children. Zechariah asked, "How can I be sure this will happen?" (Luke

1:18 NLT). Because he asked for a sign, God shut his mouth for nine months.

What was the difference between Gideon and Zechariah? We can't know for sure. God knew their hearts. Perhaps Gideon was saying, "It's not You I don't trust. I'm not sure I understand how I am capable of carrying out this seemingly impossible task. But I do believe in You, Lord."

Zechariah, on the other hand, was a high priest who had spent his life studying the Scriptures and serving in the temple. He should have trusted God because he knew the character of God.

We must tread softly when asking God to prove Himself. When we ask God to give us clear direction—whom to marry, how to proceed with a medical diagnosis, when to move on from a career, how to handle a parenting dilemma—we must come before Him in a posture of complete trust in His power, goodness, and wisdom.

Are you trusting God with what He's placed in your life today?

PRAYER:

*Lord, help me to trust You with the challenges and blessings You give to me. Thank You for the work You're doing in my life. In Jesus' name, amen.*

To trust God
in the light is nothing,
but trust Him in the dark—
THAT IS FAITH.

— CHARLES SPURGEON —

# THE STRANGER INSIDE

*I do not understand what I do.*
*For what I want to do I do not do, but what I hate I do.*

**ROMANS 7:15 NIV**

These words of the apostle Paul could be the official motto of "the morning after."

They perfectly capture the regret, disgust, and bewilderment that come from realizing—yet again—that our best intentions don't always produce the best results. That the habit we said we were done with wasn't done with us. That the resolve we prided ourselves on wasn't quite as strong as we thought. That our defense still needs a ton of help.

We can take some comfort in knowing that our struggles put us in good company. Paul wrote a good chunk of the New Testament. He possessed a fearsome intelligence and understood spiritual truths that were beyond the grasp of most other people. Yet his own failings were a mystery to him.

How was that possible? How could someone who understood so much and who taught such profound truths ultimately not understand himself? Maybe it comes down to humility. If Paul had understood his own inner workings, he might have been tempted to believe he could fix himself. That he could make the necessary tweaks for success in resisting temptation and making spiritually healthy choices. But because he didn't understand, he had to rely on Someone who did. He needed a Savior to do what he couldn't do. And so do we.

At the heart of Paul's mystification with himself was a spirit of confession and repentance. He didn't know why he was doing what he was doing, but he knew it was wrong. And he knew it was keeping him from experiencing all that God had in store for him.

So he confessed and repented to the One who understood everything about him. And in the process, he showed us how to restore our relationship with the One whose opinion of us matters most.

### PRAYER:

*Thank You, Father, for working in my conscience to remind me that I belong to You. Let me continue to find my hope in Jesus even when I see the ugliness of my old nature. In Jesus' name, amen.*

# JUST SAY YES

*Hear, O Israel: The LORD our God, the LORD is one!*
*You shall love the LORD your God with all your heart,*
*with all your soul, and with all your strength.*

**DEUTERONOMY 6:4–5 NKJV**

Extraordinary things happen when you sacrifice personal gain for the greater good.

The best coaches build winning programs based on that concept. The best drill sergeants build combat-ready soldiers based on it.

For it to work, however, the one making the sacrifice must have an unblinking trust in the one demanding the sacrifice. That's the kind of trust Moses called for in Deuteronomy 6. Jewish people refer to this passage by a single word, *Shema*, which means "to hear"—more specifically, "to hear with the intent to obey." The idea is to say yes to God before we even know what He's going to ask.

Doing this requires a special kind of faith. The purest form of trust. One that presupposes infallible wisdom and goodness on the part of the One doing the asking.

Though it may seem like a risk to sacrifice what we want for the sake of what God wants, it's actually the surest bet we'll ever be offered. God has proven Himself too many times for us not to trust His character and His design for us.

This type of faith takes practice, like a quarterback working on timing patterns with his wide receivers. We have to work on it over and over and over again until it becomes automatic. When we fail, we have to line up and try again until obeying becomes more natural than disobeying.

But it all starts with the simple decision to say yes to God.

### PRAYER:

*I fail so often in my practice, Lord,*
*that it seems like I blow it more than I succeed.*
*Thank You for Your abundant patience and forgiveness.*
*In Jesus' name, amen.*

# HEART HEALTHY

*My heart is confident in You, O God;*
*my heart is confident. No wonder I can sing Your praises.*

PSALM 57:7 NLT

We know all too well the medical strategies for maintaining a healthy heart. Eat right. Exercise. See your doctor regularly.

But what about spiritual strategies? A healthy spiritual heart is focused on God, His Word, His work in this world, and His will for His people. A healthy spiritual heart is purposeful in its approach to Bible study, prayer, and worship.

You can increase your spiritual heart health by giving yourself time and space to reflect on God. Temporarily remove yourself from the scrum of responsibilities and diversions that battle for your attention. Embrace solitude and silence. Free yourself from distractions so that you can focus on God and His Word.

You can increase your spiritual heart health by immersing yourself in Jesus' story. Start in the Gospels, the eyewitness accounts of Jesus' life. Work your way back to the Old

Testament prophets, godly men and women who predicted Jesus' coming hundreds of years before His birth. Look at what the other New Testament writers—especially the apostle Paul—say about Jesus' life, death, and resurrection, and what they mean for believers today.

You can increase your spiritual heart health by praying. Ask God's Holy Spirit to give you the wisdom to understand the Scripture passages you read and apply their principles to your life. Ask Him to help you prepare for the journey ahead, to make you receptive to the life-changing spiritual truths that await you in your study.

You can increase your spiritual heart health by finding like-minded people to accompany you on your journey. Join a Bible study group. Meet with an accountability partner. Spend quality time with mature, thoughtful Christians. Share your thoughts, feelings, and experiences. Give one another comfort, encouragement, and motivation.

### PRAYER:

*Thank You, Father, for the healthy spiritual options that are available to me every day. Keep me mindful of my heart's spiritual health so that I can grow closer to You. In Jesus' name, amen.*

# THE LEAST OF THESE

*Those who oppress the poor insult their Maker,*
*but helping the poor honors Him.*
PROVERBS 14:31 NLT

People love to claim God as one of their own. Sports fans are especially notorious. Maybe you've seen T-shirts that declare "God is a Steelers fan" or "God loves the Cowboys." The notion is ridiculous, of course. (If He rooted for anyone, wouldn't it be the Saints?)

There are, however, certain groups of people that God is a *big* fan of—people He cares about so deeply that He actually identifies Himself with them, in effect making Himself one with them.

In Matthew 25:34–40, Jesus says, "I was hungry. . . . I was thirsty. . . . I was a stranger. . . . I was naked. . . . I was sick. . . . I was in prison." He commends the people who cared for Him in His time of need and calls them "blessed."

His words of praise were met with confusion:

*Then these righteous ones will reply, "Lord, when did we ever see You hungry and feed You? Or thirsty and give You something to drink? Or a stranger and show You hospitality? Or naked and give You clothing? When did we ever see You sick or in prison and visit You?"*

*And the King will say, "I tell you the truth, when you did it to one of the least of these My brothers and sisters, you were doing it to Me!"*

Depending on your point of view, these words of Jesus may be seen as a warning or an opportunity. Certainly, they are cause for alarm for anyone who mistreats or ignores the outcasts of society. On the other hand, the chance to serve God by serving those who are dear to Him should not be taken lightly.

### PRAYER:

*Thank You for giving me the opportunity to serve You by serving others. Open my eyes to the needs of the people around me and show me how I can help meet them. In Jesus' name, amen.*

# WHAT, ME WORRY?

*Anxiety in a man's heart weighs him down,*
*but a good word makes him glad.*

PROVERBS 12:25 ESV

One day a follower of Jesus tried to involve the Lord in a dispute he was having with his brother over an inheritance. Jesus refused to arbitrate the matter. Instead, He seized the opportunity to make a bigger point about the pursuit of future security—financial and otherwise.

> *Then, turning to his disciples, Jesus said, "That is why I tell you not to worry about everyday life—whether you have enough food to eat or enough clothes to wear. For life is more than food, and your body more than clothing. Look at the ravens. They don't plant or harvest or store food in barns, for God feeds them. And you are far more valuable to Him than any birds! Can all your worries add a single moment to your life? And if worry can't accomplish a little thing like that, what's the use of worrying over bigger things?" (Luke 12:22–26 NLT)*

This isn't a blanket condemnation of those who worry. It's an appeal to His followers' wisdom and common sense. A wise person recognizes the necessary limits of his self-reliance. A wise person knows when a situation is beyond his ability to control or even effect a change. A wise person is aware of God's track record as a caretaker—His superior qualifications and experience in dealing with matters big and small. A wise person places his future in God's hands and trusts that He will do something extraordinary with it.

Jesus issues an open invitation to His followers to give their concerns and fears to His heavenly Father, who stands ready to ease their minds and lighten their burdens.

### PRAYER:

*Thank You for Your promise to ease my burden of worry. Give me the wisdom to recognize when I need to turn something over to You. In Jesus' name, amen.*

# INVESTING FOR
# THE LONG TERM

*"Don't store up treasures here on earth, where moths eat them and rust destroys them, and where thieves break in and steal. Store your treasures in heaven, where moths and rust cannot destroy, and thieves do not break in and steal. Wherever your treasure is, there the desires of your heart will also be."*

**MATTHEW 6:19–21 NLT**

As long-term investment tips go, Jesus' advice is the gold standard against which all others are measured.

He makes two key points. First, there's no such thing as a secure earthly investment. Any possession—or hobby or passion—can be taken away, through human misdeeds or natural occurrence. Those that aren't taken away tend to lose their luster or depreciate over time.

Second, even if an earthly investment *could* be secured, pouring resources into it still would make little sense in the long term. Such an investment would yield sixty to seventy years of returns at most. An investment in God's heavenly kingdom, on the other hand, has no limits on its yield. It will pay dividends forever.

You can store your treasures in heaven by building a portfolio of God-honoring work; investing in the lives of others, especially those in need; pouring your resources—money, time, and talents—into things that benefit God's kingdom; and divesting yourself of the greedy impulses that tempt you to pursue immediate gratification.

The fruitlessness of pursuing wealth and acquiring possessions is often summarized in a single phrase: "You can't take it with you." But Jesus says you *can* take it with you, if you invest your resources according to His strategy.

PRAYER:

*Thank You, Father, for the opportunity to build an eternal portfolio. Help me recognize the things that are truly valuable so that I can focus my time and attention on them. In Jesus' name, amen.*

# THE POWER OF WEAKNESS

*But He said to me, "My grace is sufficient for you,*
*for My power is made perfect in weakness."*
*Therefore I will boast all the more gladly about my weaknesses,*
*so that Christ's power may rest on me. That is why,*
*for Christ's sake, I delight in weaknesses, in insults,*
*in hardships, in persecutions, in difficulties.*
*For when I am weak, then I am strong.*

II CORINTHIANS 12:9–10 NIV

Conventional wisdom says weaknesses and struggles should be downplayed or hidden. Better to present a strong facade than to risk vulnerability.

The Bible, on the other hand, says there's great benefit to owning our weaknesses and struggles. As Paul pointed out, Jesus' power is most clearly seen in our weakness. He leaves no doubt about who's responsible for our cleared hurdles, improved relationships, solved problems, changed attitudes, renewed spirits, sudden strength, or transformed lives.

You can make your life ready for Jesus' transformation by conducting a self-exam of your thoughts, attitudes, and actions. Do you have any habits you try to hide from others?

Do you wrestle with doubt? Do you struggle with certain temptations? Do you ever put up a brave front when you feel anything but brave?

Invite the Holy Spirit's input in the process. Ask the Lord to open your eyes to blind spots in your life—areas where your weaknesses are hidden. Let the Holy Spirit work through your conscience to make you aware of things in your life that are beyond your ability to fix or change alone.

Identify enablers that make it easy for you to give in to temptation, indulge in a destructive behavior, or ignore a glaring weakness in your life. A spouse or friend who looks the other way when you overindulge or who downplays the seriousness of your behavior is an enabler. A jam-packed schedule that leaves little time for spiritual reflection is an enabler. A routine that exposes you to hard-to-resist temptations is an enabler.

Involve caring loved ones. Don't keep your personal struggles personal. Open them up to a select group, a cheering section, a support team. Make yourself accountable to trusted people who know you well and have a vested interest in your spiritual well-being.

## PRAYER:

*Father, I give my weaknesses and struggles to You. Work through them to make Yourself known to others. In Jesus' name, amen.*

# WHO, ME?

*"How can I rescue Israel?*
*My clan is the weakest in the whole tribe of Manasseh,*
*and I am the least in my entire family!"*

JUDGES 6:15 NLT

The Israelites had suffered at the hands of the Midianites and Amalekites for years. They desperately needed a hero—a warrior, a commander-in-chief with the courage and experience to lead them in a decisive military campaign.

What God gave them was Gideon. And no one was more surprised than Gideon, as you might guess from the question he asked in the Bible verse above.

Gideon was so stunned and so uncertain of himself, in fact, that he asked for three separate miraculous signs to prove that God really wanted to use him: a fire from heaven that devoured his sacrifice, a fleece that was saturated with dew while the ground around it remained dry, and a fleece that remained dry while the ground around it was saturated with dew.

Each time, God honored Gideon's request. He gave him what he needed. He equipped him mentally and emotionally for the adventure that lay ahead.

Gideon was tasked with assembling an army to battle

the Midianites and Amalekites. He gathered 32,000 men, a sizable number, but one that paled in comparison to the combined forces of his enemies.

But God said, *That's too many—31,700 too many, to be specific.*

So while the Midianites and Amalekites slept, Gideon led *300* men—who were armed only with horns and clay pots with torches inside them—into position. At his signal, his men blew their horns and smashed their pots to reveal their burning torches.

In the resulting panic and confusion, the Midianites and Amalekites began to fight one another. Those who weren't killed in the melee scattered to faraway places. Gideon, the weakest man in the insignificant tribe of Manasseh, stood victorious.

Much has changed since Gideon's time. What hasn't changed is God's penchant for using ordinary people and equipping them with the confidence they need to accomplish extraordinary things. That's why Gideon's story still matters.

### PRAYER:

*I know, heavenly Father, that You will call me to do things that are beyond what I imagine are the limits of my abilities. Show me what I'm truly capable of. In Jesus' name, amen.*

# THE HARD KIND OF FORGIVENESS

*Jesus said, "Father, forgive them,*
*for they do not know what they are doing."*

LUKE 23:34 NIV

Genuine forgiveness is one of the greatest gifts one person can offer another. The life-changing potential of the words "I forgive you" can't be overstated.

Forgiveness is an act of will and an act of love. It springs from a place of empathy. Everyone knows what it's like to be deserving of someone's anger or disappointment. To be given forgiveness instead is an amazing experience. Followers of Jesus can testify to that fact. To become a Christian is to ask for and receive wholly undeserved forgiveness from God.

To pass that experience along to someone else is an opportunity too good to pass up. There are four things you can do to offer genuine, heartfelt forgiveness to someone who needs it—whether the person asks for it or not.

First, acknowledge your feelings. If the person's actions caused you pain or embarrassment, say so. Be honest. Don't try to downplay the event or its impact on you. By the same token, you don't want to make things uncomfortable by overstating or dwelling on your pain. Be matter-of-fact, but not accusing.

Second, consider the forgiveness you've been given. If you have trouble letting something go or offering forgiveness to someone who doesn't deserve it, think of what God has forgiven you for. Make a list of the ways you've failed God and the things you've done to ruin your relationship with Him. If you get a sense of just how much you've been forgiven for, you may be more inclined to offer forgiveness to someone else.

Third, restore your relationship. Depending on the circumstances, you may not be able to enjoy the same level of trust and camaraderie you had before your rift. But with a little work, patience, and awkwardness, you can put your relationship back together.

Fourth, let it go. Once you've forgiven someone for something, forget about it. Banish it from your conversation and encourage the other person to do the same. Resist the urge to make jokes about it or to bring it up again when you get upset with the person. Let forgiveness be the end of the story.

### PRAYER:

*Holy God, You forgave me when I didn't deserve it. Give me the strength and kindness to forgive others. In Jesus' name, amen.*

If you succeed at

# LOVING
# IMPERFECT
# PEOPLE

then it becomes plausible

that somebody could love

imperfect you.

— T. D. JAKES —

# THE END OF EVIL

*Why, O Lᴏʀᴅ, do you stand far away?*
*Why do you hide yourself in times of trouble?*

**PSALM 10:1 ESV**

The psalmist's cries for justice and action from God resonate as powerfully today as they did three thousand years ago. Though we might phrase our questions differently in modern times, the meaning is the same.

"Why, O Lord, do you let predators and abusers ruin the lives of innocent children?"

"Why do you stay silent while terrorists wreak havoc in Your name?"

"Why do you allow a small percentage of people to hoard wealth and resources while so many others face poverty, neglect, and starvation?"

The assurances of Scripture may not satisfy the bloodthirsty, but they do provide a measure of comfort to those who take the long view.

Second Peter 3:9 gives us insight into God's reasoning for delaying judgment. "The Lord isn't really being slow about

His promise, as some people think. No, He is being patient for your sake. He does not want anyone to be destroyed, but wants everyone to repent" (NLT). The Lord gives even the worst of humanity the opportunity to experience His mercy and grace.

Beyond that, God leaves no doubt as to His intent:

*"I will take revenge; I will pay them back. In due time their feet will slip. Their day of disaster will arrive, and their destiny will overtake them." (Deuteronomy 32:35 NLT)*

*Evil people will surely be punished, but the children of the godly will go free. (Proverbs 11:21 NLT)*

*"I, the Lord, will punish the world for its evil and the wicked for their sin. I will crush the arrogance of the proud and humble the pride of the mighty." (Isaiah 13:11 NLT)*

In short, God will deliver perfect justice according to His perfect timing. We can rest assured in that truth, even when it seems as though evil has the upper hand.

### PRAYER:

*Heavenly Father, thank You for Your assurance that evil will be punished. Help me see the big picture when I start to despair that justice will never be served. In Jesus' name, amen.*

# A ONE-OF-A-KIND SKILL SET

*Just as each one has received a gift, use it to serve others,*
*as good stewards of the varied grace of God. If anyone speaks,*
*let it be as one who speaks God's words; if anyone serves,*
*let it be from the strength God provides, so that God may*
*be glorified through Jesus Christ in everything.*
*To Him be the glory and the power forever and ever. Amen.*

I PETER 4:10-11 CSB

You possess a set of skills, knowledge, and experience that no one else on the planet can claim. Your unique skill set makes you the ideal person for certain opportunities. No one else brings to the table what you do.

The key to maximizing your potential is to understand what you have to offer and to apply your skills where they're needed most. Here are four things you can do to maximize the gifts God has given you.

First, you can ask people whose opinion you trust to help you identify your gifts. Some spiritual gifts are less obvious than others. If you're not certain where your gifts lie, talk to the people who know you best—your friends, family members, coworkers, and others who see you in a variety of settings and situations. Ask them to share the skills, abilities, and potential they see in you.

Second, talk to your pastor or a church leader about where your gifts can be put to use. Discuss the gifts you see in yourself or the gifts others see in you. Talk about how and where they can be applied. Someone who's familiar with a broad range of ministry opportunities may suggest some possibilities you've never considered before.

Third, adjust your schedule as necessary. To get involved in a ministry or take advantage of a service opportunity, you may need to sacrifice other items on your calendar. As you prioritize the things vying for your attention, consider the impact that using your spiritual gifts may have if you give yourself enough time to reach your full potential.

Fourth, encourage others to do the same. Once you've gone through the process of discovering and learning to use your own gifts, you can help friends and acquaintances do the same. Talk to other people about the gifts and abilities you see in them. Encourage them to find ways to put their skills to use.

### PRAYER:

*Heavenly Father, thank You for the unique skill set You've given me. Show me how to use my gifts in ways that will impact other people's lives. In Jesus' name, amen.*

# THE RIGHT TIMETABLE

*Wait for the L<small>ORD</small>; be strong and
let your heart take courage; yes, wait for the L<small>ORD</small>.*

**PSALM 27:14 NASB**

Abraham and Sarah had a *promise*. The Lord had vowed that one day Abraham's descendants would be as numerous as the stars in the sky.

Abraham and Sarah had a *problem*. They were childless. He was in his mid-eighties. She was in her mid-seventies.

Abraham and Sarah had a *choice*. They could wait for God to do what He promised—or they could take an active role in *making* His promise come true.

Abraham and Sarah had a *solution*. Sarah owned an Egyptian servant named Hagar, who was in her prime childbearing years. Sarah proposed that Abraham impregnate Hagar so that they could raise their servant's child as their own.

Not content to rely on God and operate by His timetable, they chose instead to rely on their own cleverness and force the issue. Their plan worked—all too well. Hagar conceived and delivered Abraham's child, a boy named Ishmael. Not surprisingly, tensions ran high among father, birth mother, and would-be adoptive mother. And when Sarah herself became pregnant and gave birth to a son, Isaac, years later, the situation became unbearable. Hagar and Ishmael were cast aside, sent away by Abraham into the desert to fend for themselves. God, however, did not abandon them. He provided water for them and promised Hagar that Ishmael's descendants would be a great nation (see Genesis 21).

The story of Abraham and Sarah continues a theme that runs throughout Scripture and extends to believers today. Those who are content to rely on the Lord and operate according to His timetable are richly rewarded. Those, on the other hand, who rely on themselves or attempt to manipulate God's timetable—regardless of how noble their intentions may seem—find that the consequences of their actions soon snowball beyond their control.

The last word on the subject belongs to the author of Lamentations, who observed, "The Lord is good to those who wait for Him" (3:25 NKJV).

### PRAYER:

*Father, thank You for Your perfect timing.*
*Give me the wisdom to recognize it. In Jesus' name, amen.*

# THE MOST IMPORTANT QUESTION

*What shall I do, then, with Jesus who is called the Messiah?*

MATTHEW 27:22 NIV

**A**fter Jesus' arrest, the Roman governor Pilate was taken aback by the reaction of the Jewish crowd. In keeping with Passover tradition, Pilate had offered to free a prisoner. The crowd was given the choice of freeing Barabbas, a notorious criminal, or Jesus, an innocent man. Prompted by Jewish religious leaders, the crowd overwhelmingly chose to free Barabbas.

Pilate's next question was inevitable: What shall I do with Jesus?

Two thousand years later, people are asking the same question.

We've heard Jesus' name invoked from all sides of hot-button political, social, and religious issues. We've been told to consider what He would do in given situations. We've heard Him described as a teacher, a prophet, a legend, a revolutionary, the Son of God, and the Savior, among other things. It's only natural that we have questions about Him.

The first thing to do is tackle the question "What shall I do with Jesus?" in your own life. What was your attitude toward

Him in the past? What, if anything, made you reconsider your position? What have been the results? If you can answer those questions for yourself, you may be able to help other people sort through their feelings.

The second thing is to turn to the Bible. The Gospels contain several stories of people who dismissed or underestimated Jesus—until they encountered Him. The evidence of these change-of-heart stories can be persuasive to people looking for answers.

The third thing is to anticipate opposing views. Some people carry preconceived notions about Jesus that rob them of any desire or interest in investigating Him further. Those notions may be based on previous encounters with Christians, personal tragedies they blame on God, or the prejudices of others. The more you understand various opinions about Jesus, the better prepared you'll be to address them. Talk to your pastor or a mature Christian about how to anticipate opposing views.

### PRAYER:

*Heavenly Father, thank You for the opportunity to consider— again and again—Jesus' place in my life. Give me the wisdom to help others who struggle with answering the question Pilate asked. In Jesus' name, amen.*

# AGREE TO DISAGREE

*Don't have anything to do with foolish and stupid arguments,
because you know they produce quarrels.*

II TIMOTHY 2:23 NIV

Defending one's political, moral, or spiritual beliefs has become a blood sport in our culture. Television news shows, talk radio stations, and social media sites have turned into brutal verbal battlefields. Some attacks are so vicious, so vitriolic, that the knee-jerk reaction is to respond with an equal level of venom. Anything less, it seems, is tantamount to surrender.

In the end, though, little is accomplished by such responses, aside from sacrificing biblical principles. The potential damage from being too zealous in defending Christian ideals and principles is sobering.

The Bible gives us guidelines that sanction these kinds of interactions—guidelines that hold believers to high standards in dealing with antagonists.

"Better to hear the quiet words of a wise person than the shouts of a foolish king" (Ecclesiastes 9:17 NLT). Quiet words are words that don't inspire anger in others. Quiet words ease antagonism and allow real dialogue to occur.

"Words from the mouth of the wise are gracious, but fools are consumed by their own lips" (Ecclesiastes 10:12 NIV). Gracious words acknowledge the worth of people you disagree with. Recognizing people's value makes it more difficult to insult or attack them later.

"God blesses you when people mock you and persecute you and lie about you and say all sorts of evil things against you because you are My followers. Be happy about it! Be very glad! For a great reward awaits you in heaven. And remember, the ancient prophets were persecuted in the same way" (Matthew 5:11–12 NLT). Sometimes being attacked for holding a certain view or defending a certain Christian principle is a badge of honor. There's no need to defend ourselves.

## PRAYER:

*Heavenly Father, my tongue is an unpredictable weapon, capable of doing damage that I'm not even aware of. Give me the discipline to speak in the way You would have me speak. In Jesus' name, amen.*

# GREAT EXPECTATIONS

*You shall love the Lord your God with all your heart
and with all your soul and with all your mind. This is
the great and first commandment. And a second is like it:
You shall love your neighbor as yourself.*

MATTHEW 22:37-39 ESV

Life-changing introspection begins with a single question: *What does God want from me?* Once you understand His expectations, you can take steps to fulfill them.

The ideal starting point is the passage above, in which Jesus identifies the greatest commandment in the Law—the most important instruction for God's people to obey.

Love God and love others.

So simple, yet so challenging, because Jesus isn't talking about the *emotion* of love. He's not talking about loving *feelings* that ebb and flow depending on circumstances and mood. He's talking about the *practice* of love—demonstrating deep and abiding concern for others through sacrificial and loving deeds.

If your goal is to embrace God's expectations for your life, here are a few ideas to get you started. First, read case studies in the Bible. Look closely at the way God interacts with people. Pay particular attention to how He makes

Himself known, equips them for the task at hand, puts them in positions to use their gifts and abilities, and deals with their doubts and setbacks.

Second, talk to a trusted Christian adviser. Sometimes an outsider's perspective can reveal aspects of yourself that you've never noticed. Throughout Scripture, God uses other people to communicate or confirm His will. The key is to find someone you trust, someone who knows you well and is committed to God's work.

Third, choose one or two areas to focus on first. Trying to do too much too soon can take a toll. Once you have a sense of what God's expectations are, you can plot a step-by-step strategy for meeting them. For example, your first step might involve learning to control your temper or getting more involved in other people's lives. Once you've done that, you can move on to the next step.

Fourth, journal your results. Keep track of your successes and failures. Make sure you understand what you did right in certain circumstances and what you did wrong in others so that you can build on your successes and avoid repeating your mistakes.

### PRAYER:

*Father, my goal is to fulfill Your expectations.*
*Show me how. In Jesus' name, amen.*

# DEFYING EXPECTATIONS

*A very large crowd spread their cloaks on the road,*
*while others cut branches from the trees and spread them*
*on the road. The crowds that went ahead of Him and those*
*that followed shouted, "Hosanna to the Son of David!"*
*"Blessed is He who comes in the name of the Lord!"*
*"Hosanna in the highest heaven!"*

MATTHEW 21:8-9 NIV

To see Jesus for who He really is, we have to leave our expectations behind.

The crowd that gathered to welcome the Lord to Jerusalem five days before His death certainly learned that lesson. At that time, Israel was part of the Roman Empire—a political reality the people of Israel desperately wanted to change. They looked to God's ancient promise of a Messiah, a Savior, for comfort. They believed this chosen One of God would lead them in revolt against Rome and establish a sovereign Jewish nation.

Excitement overflowed as Jesus slowly made His way through the main thoroughfare of the city. People laid palm branches on the road as a gesture of respect and honor. Was this the king, come to claim His throne? Yes—and no.

The Bible makes it clear that Jesus was indeed the Messiah, the King whom God had promised in the Old Testament. But His kingdom was nothing like what the people expected. Jesus' kingdom was spiritual, not political (John 18:36). His enemies were sin and the forces of darkness in this world, not the Roman Empire.

When it became apparent that Jesus wasn't going to lead a military attack on Rome, the people turned on Him. Spurred on by Jewish religious leaders, they called for His execution. Five days after His triumphant arrival, Jesus was crucified.

Yet death could not stop Jesus from ushering in His kingdom. According to Scripture, His kingdom grows in the hearts of everyone who follows Him (Matthew 13:1–23).

### PRAYER:

*Heavenly Father, thank You for sending Your Son to accomplish the work of salvation. Help me leave behind my expectations so that I can see Jesus for who He really is. In His name, amen.*

# SACRIFICE

*He Himself brought our sins in His body up on the cross,*
*so that we might die to sin and live for righteousness;*
*by His wounds you were healed.*

**I PETER 2:24 NASB**

**W**hen people talk about Jesus' sacrifice, they tend to focus on His suffering and death. Yet Jesus' sacrifice began the moment He took human form.

Remember, Jesus is the One who spoke the universe into existence. He breathed life into us. He possessed all the attributes of God. His presence dwarfed the universe. His power and knowledge were limitless. Nothing could harm Him.

Yet He willingly came to earth to dwell among His creation as a human being. He left His idyllic existence in heaven for a life of rejection, ridicule, and betrayal on a sin-ravaged planet. He became a helpless baby, dependent on others. He made Himself vulnerable to pain, sickness, exhaustion, humiliation, and eventually death. He squeezed His infinite presence into a casing of flesh.

During His earthly ministry, Jesus gave up the comforts of home and family to share His Good News with as many people as possible. He gave up His time and energy to teach, heal, comfort, and challenge others.

Jesus' ministry involved a tremendous personal cost to Him. He was willing to pay that cost for one reason: love. "This is how we know what love is: Jesus Christ laid down His life for us. And we ought to lay down our lives for our brothers and sisters" (I John 3:16 NIV).

Before Jesus laid down His life on the cross, He laid it down in hundreds, even thousands, of smaller ways. A verbal encouragement here. A healing touch there. A constructive reprimand. A social visit. A word of insight into God's nature. A loving gaze that said, "You may feel overlooked by society, but I see you. I know you. You have value. You are precious to Me."

Such instances of everyday love and sacrifice can resonate for a lifetime. That's why, throughout Scripture, Jesus' followers are urged to follow His example of loving sacrifice.

### PRAYER:

*Father, I can never thank You enough for the sacrifice of Your Son—but I can honor it by sacrificing for others. Help me make the most of my opportunities to do that. In Jesus' name, amen.*

# JUST PERFECT

*For God made Christ, who never sinned,*
*to be the offering for our sin, so that*
*we could be made right with God through Christ.*

**II CORINTHIANS 5:21 NLT**

In His thirty-three years on earth, Jesus did not sin. Every decision He made, every word He spoke, every action He took honored His Father in heaven. He—alone in the annals of human history—lived a life that was perfectly righteous in God's eyes.

According to Matthew 4:1–11, Satan himself tempted Jesus in an intense one-on-one encounter, but he could not persuade Him to deviate from God's will. A few years later, the accusers at Jesus' trial had to invent charges to level against Him. They could find no legitimate offenses of which to accuse Him.

In theological terms, Jesus' perfection was an absolute necessity. Humankind's sins demanded punishment in the form of a sacrifice. But only a perfect sacrifice was acceptable to God. Because Jesus was blameless in His thoughts, words, and deeds—perfect in every way—He met God's requirements. He who was without sin, innocent of everything the human race was guilty of, was the only One who could pay the price for our sin.

In personal terms, Jesus' perfection paves the way for a lifelong—and life-changing—dialogue with everyone who follows Him. The author of Hebrews presents the case clearly: "For we do not have a high priest who is unable to empathize with our weaknesses, but we have one who has been tempted in every way, just as we are—yet He did not sin" (Hebrews 4:15 NIV).

Jesus knows what it's like to be tempted to take a moral shortcut, to ignore spiritual responsibilities, and to let emotions dictate a response. More to the point, He knows how to recognize those temptations for what they are, how to lessen their power, and how to make the best decisions in any given circumstance. He stands ready to come alongside and share His wisdom and strength with anyone who strives to follow His perfect example.

### PRAYER:

*Father, though Jesus is perfect and I am far from perfect, there's nothing I will ever experience that He doesn't understand. Never let me forget that. In Jesus' name, amen.*

Look for Christ
and you will find Him,
and with Him
EVERYTHING
ELSE.

— C. S. LEWIS —

# THE ONE WHO NOTICED

*When He saw the crowds, He had compassion on them, because they were harassed and helpless, like sheep without a shepherd.*

MATTHEW 9:36 NIV

Crowds flocked to Jesus because they could sense His concern. They were changed by His words and healed by His power, but they were touched first by His compassion.

Jesus' compassion began with noticing. "As He went along, He saw a man blind from birth" (John 9:1 NIV). In first-century Israel, people who suffered from blindness or other afflictions were virtually invisible. They frequently gathered near the temple to beg money from kindhearted worshipers. They were usually ignored, however, because people believed their condition was God's punishment for some sin they or their parents had committed.

Jesus refused to ignore the blind man. He didn't stare straight ahead to avoid an awkward encounter. He looked at him and took note of his condition and needs. He made a connection.

Jesus didn't just notice people; He also empathized with them. When He visited His friends Mary and Martha after the death of their brother, Lazarus, His plan was to raise Lazarus from the dead. Jesus knew that soon Lazarus would be alive again.

Yet when Jesus saw the mourners who had gathered, anguished and devastated by Lazarus's death, He wept (John 11:35). He put Himself in their place, felt their pain, and reacted with empathy. He didn't just observe their suffering; He joined them in it.

Jesus also intervened when He saw people in need. He gave sight to the blind man in John 9. He brought Lazarus back to life. He also removed disabilities, healed all manner of sickness, and freed people from demon possession. Yet not all of His interventions were miraculous. In John 8, He protected a woman from a crowd of men who threatened to stone her to death for adultery. In Luke 19, He socialized with a despised tax collector and his socially unacceptable friends.

In each situation, Jesus acted on someone else's behalf. That's His legacy of compassion. He stepped into people's lives, acquainted Himself with their circumstances, and took steps to meet their needs.

Those who choose to follow Him have a blueprint for impacting people's lives in similar ways.

## PRAYER:

*Father, the compassion of Your Son changed countless lives. Guide my attempts to show the same kind of compassion to others. In Jesus' name, amen.*

# OVERWHELMED

*Now go, for I am sending you to Pharaoh.*
*You must lead My people Israel out of Egypt.*

EXODUS 3:10 NLT

**Job Description**

- Negotiating the release of two million Israelite slaves from a hostile government
- Leading them on a journey across a barren wilderness to invade an occupied nation
- Seeing to their physical, emotional, social, and spiritual needs during the journey
- Preparing people with no military experience for warfare against powerful enemies
- Meeting one-on-one with God Himself
- Performing miracles as needed

*Previous Experience:* Shepherd

Do you see a match there? God did. He chose Moses, a man who had been tending sheep for forty years, to rescue His people from four hundred years of slavery in Egypt.

Understandably, Moses was overwhelmed by his new responsibilities. His first reaction was to ask God to send someone else. To ease Moses' mind, God let him take along his brother, Aaron, to confront Pharaoh and demand the release of the Israelites. God understood how daunting the task seemed to the poor shepherd.

It could be argued that aside from Jesus Christ, no one in the Bible was asked to do more than Moses. His responsibilities might have taken a serious toll on his physical and emotional health, if it weren't for a three-pronged strategy he used to deal with them. This simple but effective strategy is every bit as applicable today as it was 2,500 years ago.

First, he designated responsibilities. Like many people faced with an overwhelming task, Moses' first instinct was to micromanage. The wise counsel of his father-in-law helped him realize he shouldn't try to do everything himself. So Moses recruited capable people to oversee certain areas so that he could concentrate on the big picture.

Second, he leaned on people he trusted. His brother, Aaron, and sister, Miriam, became trusted advisers. He didn't have to wonder about their loyalty or ulterior motives. Moses understood that peace of mind helps you operate at your full potential.

Third, he poured out his feelings and frustrations to the Lord. The only One who could truly empathize with Moses was God Himself, so that's where Moses turned to vent his frustrations and get his marching orders.

### PRAYER:

*Father, You recognize potential in me that I can't see.*
*Give me the confidence to fulfill that potential and the humility*
*to lean on You every step of the way. In Jesus' name, amen.*

# SHREWD AND INNOCENT

*I am sending you out like sheep among wolves.*
*Therefore be as shrewd as snakes and as innocent as doves.*

MATTHEW 10:16 NIV

This is the sobering advice Jesus gave His disciples before He sent them to carry out His ministry. He wanted them to understand that they were going to face opposition, resistance, and persecution. And He wanted them to face it with a demeanor that would make an impression.

Being "innocent as doves" means turning the other cheek, going the extra mile, and showing love to your enemies. It means conducting yourself in a way that's above reproach and not giving your opponents ammunition against you.

What it *doesn't* mean is being naive. Hence, Jesus' instruction to be "as shrewd as snakes." Shrewdness—the ability to understand things and make good judgments—can be developed in different ways.

You can develop it by learning to discern people's motives and intent. Jesus provided an excellent model of this. He knew when His enemies were trying to trap Him. He saw through their faux respectfulness and seemingly sincere questions. In fact, He often confronted them about their evil intent.

You can develop shrewdness by recognizing how you're being perceived. For better or worse, many people hold some rather strong opinions about followers of Jesus. The more you know about their opinions and preconceived notions, the better equipped you'll be to handle—and perhaps even change—them.

You can develop shrewdness by anticipating opposition and debate. Jesus warned that His faithful followers would face adversity. It's not a question of *if*, but *when*. Knowing this gives you a chance to prepare. Girding yourself for battle by studying God's Word or discussing strategy with other trusted believers will make you a formidable opponent.

The guidelines Jesus gave His disciples in Matthew 10 still apply today. The nature of the opposition has changed, but the expectations remain. The most effective ambassadors for Christ are shrewd as snakes and innocent as doves.

## PRAYER:

*Father, thank You for entrusting me with Jesus' ministry. Guide my efforts to be innocent and shrewd in my interactions with other people. In Jesus' name, amen.*

# BUILD WISELY

*Everyone who hears these words of Mine and acts on them will be like a wise man who built his house on the rock. The rain fell, the rivers rose, and the winds blew and pounded that house. Yet it didn't collapse, because its foundation was on the rock. But everyone who hears these words of Mine and doesn't act on them will be like a foolish man who built his house on the sand. The rain fell, the rivers rose, the winds blew and pounded that house, and it collapsed. It collapsed with a great crash.*

MATTHEW 7:24–27 CSB

Few people purposely build their lives on an unstable foundation. The problem lies in determining what is truly stable. Some things—financial security, a personal philosophy, the promise of comfort—seem solid at first glance. They invite us to stake a claim on them.

The temptation is to trust that their stability will continue and so begin to build a life on them. Proverbs 16:25 warns about this temptation: "There is a way that appears to be right, but in the end it leads to death" (NIV).

The problem is, many of these foundations don't reveal themselves to be unreliable until life's storms hit. Only then do you realize the foolishness of building on them. And by then, it's too late.

That's why Jesus recommended Himself and His teachings as a foundation. As the Son of God, He is able to offer the Creator and Sustainer of the universe as security for His promises. As long as God exists, Jesus' promises and teachings can be trusted. And the foundation He offers will remain rock-solid.

### PRAYER:

*Father, thank You for giving me a Bedrock*
*on which to build my life.*
*Remind me that I can stand firm*
*when the storms of life rage.*
*In Jesus' name, amen.*

# CHOOSE
# YOUR BATTLES

*Understand this, my dear brothers and sisters:*
*You must all be quick to listen, slow to speak,*
*and slow to get angry.*

JAMES 1:19 NLT

On the night Jesus was arrested, His disciple Peter cut off a man's ear trying to protect Him. Peter thought he was being heroic, until Jesus set him straight. Jesus rebuked Peter, healed the injured man, and allowed Himself to be led away, in obedience to God's plan.

Peter was left to ponder his decision. He chose a battle in the heat of the moment and ended up disappointing Jesus. His story serves as a warning to all believers.

When conflict arises, we must ask, "Is this worth fighting for?" Every confrontation exacts a price. Strained relationships and a damaged reputation are two of the costs. The more we engage in combative behavior, the more damage we cause.

We must learn to understand opposing views. If we know what our opponents believe and why, we can have a more thoughtful and informed interaction. Making an effort to understand an opposing view demonstrates empathy and curiosity. It may also inspire your opponents to investigate your point of view.

We must resist the urge to "win." Too often competitiveness drives the interaction between believers and those who oppose them. The desire to win, to prove superiority, stiffens resolve and causes both sides to dig in that much harder. What otherwise might have been a constructive dialogue in which both parties come away understanding each other a little better instead becomes a fight to the finish, a constant search for openings in which to attack.

We must consider the circumstances. Is the person on the other side of the argument defending a principle or speaking from a deep (and possibly painful) personal experience? No debate is worth causing a hurting person to suffer more.

We must "speak the truth in love" (Ephesians 4:15 NLT). No matter how infuriating a person's beliefs may be, our first responsibility is to show the person loving-kindness. Our aim is to speak from the heart in a way that leaves our opponents feeling affirmed—and a little curious about a faith that encourages loving one's opponents.

### PRAYER:
*Father, my goal is to defend Your truth without doing harm to Your kingdom. Give me wisdom in choosing my battles. In Jesus' name, amen.*

# STEP UP

*Near the cross of Jesus stood His mother, His mother's sister,*
*Mary the wife of Clopas, and Mary Magdalene.*
*When Jesus saw His mother there, and the disciple*
*whom He loved standing nearby, He said to her,*
*"Woman, here is your son," and to the disciple,*
*"Here is your mother." From that time on,*
*this disciple took her into his home.*

JOHN 19:25–27 NIV

Jesus gave His disciple John an extraordinary opportunity to do something for Him—to ease His suffering by agreeing to take care of Mary.

This wasn't a spur-of-the-moment decision on Jesus' part. He reached out to John because He knew John's character and heart. He knew John was the best person for the job.

To John's credit, he recognized that too. When the spotlight fell on him and the opportunity to serve presented itself, he didn't hesitate. He stepped up to assume the responsibilities laid out before him. And in the process, he set a powerful example for all of Jesus' followers.

If you want to be someone people look to in times of need or crisis, you can prepare by building a reputation for yourself one encounter at a time. Lay a foundation of honesty, kindness, and compassion in your dealings with others.

You can put yourself in the right place at the right time. Make yourself available to people in need. Prove yourself to be a conscientious worker and someone with a servant's heart. Spend time regularly in service settings, using your gifts to help others.

You can say yes to a responsibility that scares you a little. Step out of your comfort zone. Introduce yourself to people outside your circle of acquaintances. Take on a task that challenges you. God knows what you're capable of; you need to find out as well. There's a world of service just waiting to open up to you.

### PRAYER:

*Father, I want to be someone to whom people look in times of crisis. Give me the courage to step out of my comfort zone and exercise my servant's heart. In Jesus' name, amen.*

# STAND FIRM

*Anyone who offers a prayer to any god or person besides you,*
*O king, for thirty days, shall be thrown into the lions' den.*

DANIEL 6:7 NASB

From the time he was taken captive by the Babylonians, Daniel had made a name for himself as a trusted adviser to King Darius. His sudden rise in Darius's government made him a marked man among the king's other advisers. Yet Daniel had proven himself adept at negotiating palace intrigue.

Some things, however, were nonnegotiable.

A faction of rogue advisers crafted a decree (quoted above) that was nothing more than a shrewd political maneuver—a way for Daniel's enemies to force his hand. But the king didn't know that when he made it law. He didn't know that his favorite adviser prayed three times a day to the God of Israel—in front of an open window that faced Jerusalem.

When Daniel heard about the new law, he went straight to his room and prayed to God, in full view of his enemies, who were watching.

The rest of the story is well-documented. Darius, much to his distress, was forced to throw Daniel into a pit of starved lions and seal the pit with a stone. At the first light of dawn, he rushed back to the pit and called out to Daniel, who responded: "O king, live forever! My God sent His angel and shut the lions' mouths, and they have not harmed me, since I was found innocent before Him; and also toward you, O king, I have committed no crime" (Daniel 6:21–22 NASB).

Darius ordered the execution of the men who had accused Daniel. He issued a new decree that everyone in his kingdom should "tremble and fear before the God of Daniel" (Daniel 6:26 NASB).

The takeaway is that standing firm for God always pays dividends. That's not to say that a miraculous outcome awaits everyone who takes a stand. Millions of Christian martyrs could testify to that fact. Yet one person's stand has the power to inspire others, to change hearts, and to produce results far beyond their immediate circumstances.

### PRAYER:

*Father, give me the courage to stand firm when it matters and the wisdom to recognize that it always matters. In Jesus' name, amen.*

# A STORY TO TELL

*You will receive power when the Holy Spirit comes on you; and you will be My witnesses in Jerusalem, and in all Judea and Samaria, and to the ends of the earth.*

ACTS 1:8 NIV

The Christian faith is an extraordinary combination of the private and the public. The decision to follow Christ is intensely personal, as it often involves deep soul-searching and difficult confession and repentance.

Yet Jesus challenges His followers to use their personal experiences in a public way to reach out and minister to others. It's a tall order, especially for introverts and people who are less than secure in their ministry skills. Yet where Jesus commands, He also equips. You can become a confident, effective witness for Jesus.

Your own experience is a great place to start. Spend some time thinking about your Christian walk—both the highs and the lows. Practice sharing your story in a concise and interesting way. Find a style and approach that's accessible and relatable. Talk about the changes in your self-image, your relationships, your outlook, and your thoughts about the future that have occurred since you started following Jesus.

You'll need to anticipate questions. Put yourself in the other person's position. If someone were telling you about Jesus, what would you ask? What objections would you raise? What obstacles might get in the way of your understanding? If you can anticipate potential reactions on the part of your listeners, you can be prepared to address them.

Make sure you can support your statements with relevant Scripture passages. The more comfortable you are with accessing those passages, the more effective your witness will be. Spend some time in God's Word, marking and learning passages you can use when you share your faith with others.

The secret to being an effective witness is knowing when to speak and when to listen, as well as knowing what to say and what *not* to say. God's Holy Spirit is your most valuable ally in this pursuit. Ask Him to guide your words so that they have the intended effect in other people's lives.

### PRAYER:

*Heavenly Father, thank You for giving me a story to tell.*
*Help me to tell it well. In Jesus' name, amen.*

# LET YOUR LIGHT SHINE

*You are the light of the world—*
*like a city on a hilltop that cannot be hidden.*
*No one lights a lamp and then puts it under a basket. Instead,*
*a lamp is placed on a stand, where it gives light to everyone*
*in the house. In the same way, let your good deeds shine out*
*for all to see, so that everyone will praise your heavenly Father.*

MATTHEW 5:14–16 NLT

How can you spot a Christian?

The question lends itself to a variety of punch lines, doesn't it? Thanks to Jesus' words in Matthew 5, the question also lends itself to some serious discussion.

The light that shines in and through a believer is the evidence of a changed life. People don't usually want to *hear* what Jesus can do; they want to *see* it. The more apparent that light is, the greater the impression it will make.

So let's rephrase the question: What does the shining

light of a Christian look like? Where can it be seen?

The possibilities are limitless. The Light of the World can be seen when a believer

- reaches out to someone who's fallen, instead of stepping over him or kicking him when he's down;
- helps others understand God's Word;
- redirects praise and glory to God;
- offers a thoughtful and loving response to a personal attack;
- maintains a spirit of thankfulness when things get rough;
- takes a genuine interest in other people's well-being;
- sacrifices his own comfort or provisions for the sake of someone else.

Jesus' point is that the right "light" in the right place at the right time can make a difference in the lives of countless people struggling in darkness.

### PRAYER:

*Father in heaven, You put the light inside me.*
*Show me how I can let it shine wherever I am.*
*In Jesus' name, amen.*

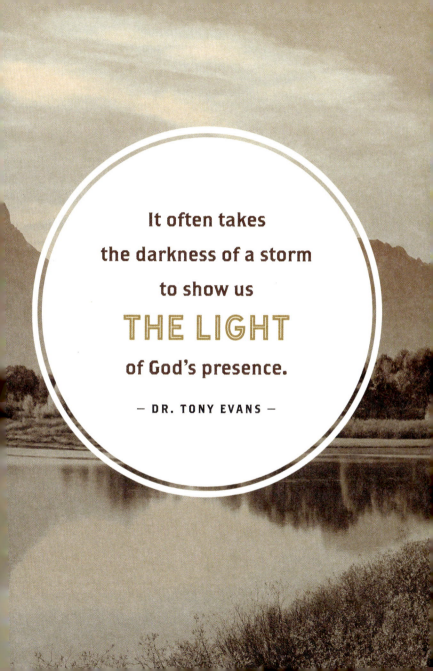

It often takes
the darkness of a storm
to show us
**THE LIGHT**
of God's presence.

— DR. TONY EVANS —

# PURE RELIGION

*Pure and genuine religion in the sight of God the Father means caring for orphans and widows in their distress and refusing to let the world corrupt you.*

JAMES 1:27 NLT

A single word can make a big difference. Notice that James uses the preposition *for*, and not *about*, in describing the kind of response that pleases God. *For* is the essence of pure and genuine religion. *About* adds an air of questionability to our faith. *About* is what inspires people to use air quotes when they say the word *religion*.

To care *about* orphans and widows in their distress is to give lip service to their needs. To bemoan their deplorable plight. To speechify about the systemic failures that allowed them to slip through the cracks of society.

In contrast, to care *for* widows and orphans is to do what nurses do *for* their patients. That is, to discover through one-on-one interaction the source of their pain or suffering and then to work to alleviate it in a hands-on way.

Pure and genuine religion is messy. It's risky. It's awkward at times. It takes Christians out of their comfort zones. It puts them in the orbit of people they might not otherwise encounter.

Pure and genuine religion requires a sacrifice of time and energy. It asks a lot of us. It takes a toll. It wears us out when we do it right. But ultimately pure and genuine religion makes a difference. It changes lives. It binds us to other people in ways nothing else can. And it pleases God.

What are some steps you can take today to move from caring *about* someone to caring *for* that person? Whom can you invite to serve alongside you?

### PRAYER:

*God in heaven, thank You for setting such a high bar for believers. Give me the strength and endurance to rise to the challenge of demonstrating pure and genuine religion to people in need. I want to care for others, not just care about them. In Jesus' name, amen.*

# GRUDGE MATCH

*So if you are offering your gift at the altar and there remember*
*that your brother has something against you,*
*leave your gift there before the altar and go.*
*First be reconciled to your brother,*
*and then come and offer your gift.*

MATTHEW 5:23-24 ESV

How long is too long to hold a grudge? You probably don't have to look hard to find people who have held grudges for years. Yet, according to Jesus' words in Matthew 5, anything longer than the time it takes to realize that you're holding a grudge is too long to hold a grudge.

If we're honest, that's bad news for a lot of us, because holding a grudge feels good. Holding a grudge makes us feel as though we have the upper hand. Because grudges usually begin with an offense that we believe has been committed against us, holding one gives us a sense of moral superiority. We feel justified in ignoring God's command to love one another. We reckon that being offended somehow releases us from the responsibility of living in a Christlike way.

But Christ Himself begs to differ.

In Matthew 5, Jesus puts reconciliation ahead of offering sacrifices to God in worship. That says something about the priority He places on loving relationships. Obstacles that get in the way of those relationships—whether they're caused by wounded pride, misunderstandings, or disagreements that snowball into something more—must be dealt with sooner rather than later.

Based on Jesus' words in Matthew, we can conclude that grudges that are allowed to fester will affect not only the relationship between the two people involved, but also their individual relationships with God.

## PRAYER:

*Father in heaven, thank You for concerning Yourself with our relationships and showing us how to live in a way that pleases You. Release my grip on the grudges I hold so that I can enjoy an uninterrupted relationship with You. In Jesus' name, amen.*

# LOVE WHOM?

*But to you who are willing to listen, I say, love your enemies!*
*Do good to those who hate you. Bless those who curse you.*
*Pray for those who hurt you. If someone slaps you on one cheek,*
*offer the other cheek also. If someone demands your coat,*
*offer your shirt also. Give to anyone who asks; and when things*
*are taken away from you, don't try to get them back.*
*Do to others as you would like them to do to you.*

LUKE 6:27-31 NLT

They are perhaps the most subversive words ever spoken. The Jewish people of Jesus' day certainly recognized the subversion in His instructions. Their enemies were the Romans, who had oppressed the Jews and made their lives miserable for decades. The implications of Jesus' words—especially His call to show loving concern for the Roman troops who occupied their land—were so radical, they bordered on treason. His expectations were so far from their normal way of thinking that many Jews simply dismissed them—and Jesus—without a second thought.

Those expectations are no less challenging today. Jesus'

instructions in Luke 6 require people to subvert their natural instincts. Getting revenge on those who have wronged you makes sense. Doing to others as they do to you feels natural. But showing *love* to enemies? Choosing a nonviolent response when someone assaults you? Going above and beyond for someone who has made your life miserable?

That's just not normal. In fact, it's extraordinary. And that's the point.

To follow Jesus' teachings is to stand out—to draw the attention of others. The person who shows love to an enemy earns the right to talk about the One who makes such a response possible.

Beyond that, showing love to enemies is the most effective means for reducing the enemy population. Love has the ability to transcend borders and ideological differences— and to transform enemies into allies.

In a time when "an eye for an eye" still dominates as the strategy for dealing with enemies, Jesus' words keep the world from going blind.

## PRAYER:

*Father, You know how hard this command is for me.*
*Do what You have to do in my heart to help me love*
*the people I really don't want to love. In Jesus' name, amen.*

# EYE EXAM

*Why do you see the speck that is in your brother's eye,*
*but do not notice the log that is in your own eye?*
*How can you say to your brother, 'Brother, let me take out*
*the speck that is in your eye,' when you yourself*
*do not see the log that is in your own eye?*
*You hypocrite, first take the log out of your own eye,*
*and then you will see clearly to take out the speck*
*that is in your brother's eye.*

LUKE 6:41–42 ESV

**H**ypocrisy is the unforgivable sin, as far as many critics of Christianity are concerned. How much emotional and spiritual damage has been caused by "religious types" who are quick to judge and slow to love? How far has the cause of Christ been set back by people who preach one thing and practice another?

Jesus' pointed words in Luke 6 were directed to people who feel the need to tell others what's wrong with them. The problem is, in doing so, they show a complete lack of awareness of their own flaws. And they become hypocrites, whether they realize it or not.

The antidote to hypocrisy is humility. Truly humble people are aware of their own shortcomings and areas of struggle. They understand how difficult it can be to overcome certain obstacles or resist certain temptations. They look at others as fellow strugglers and not suspects. Their empathy surpasses their desire to claim moral superiority.

Jesus' message is simple: If you want to be an instrument of God's grace, you must maintain an attitude of humble self-awareness. You must leave the judging to Him. You must interact with struggling people as a friend and not a prosecutor.

## PRAYER:

*Heavenly Father, I can't always see the log in my own eye. Please remind me of it the next time I start to notice the speck in someone else's eye. In Jesus' name, amen.*

# BE HUMBLE

*For those who exalt themselves will be humbled,*
*and those who humble themselves will be exalted.*

LUKE 14:11 NLT

The truth of Jesus' words is played out repeatedly in Scripture. Look at the following examples:

- Moses, a refugee on the run from a murder charge who found work as a shepherd
- Rahab, a prostitute in a pagan city
- Gideon, a man so unsure of himself that he needed three miracles to be convinced that God was calling him
- Ruth, a poor widow who survived by scrounging leftover grain in the fields
- Saul, a man so reluctant to become king that he hid from the people who were trying to anoint him
- David, the tagalong little brother of "real" warriors
- Mary, an unmarried young woman from a nondescript Jewish town
- Peter, Andrew, James, and John, blue-collar types with no formal religious training
- Paul, a man so misguided that he started his career persecuting Christians.

Each of them was used by God to accomplish something

extraordinary. And their humility was one of the key attributes that made them valuable to Him.

It comes down to a question of glory—specifically, *Who gets it?* People who are prone to exalt themselves or take a bow in God's spotlight are useless to Him. God's purpose is to reveal Himself and His power to humankind. People who don't give Him all glory and honor confuse the issue and interfere with His plan.

Those who embrace humility, on the other hand, are perfect instruments for His work. Fake humility doesn't cut it. Neither does self-degradation. The humility Jesus is talking about involves recognizing that all of our talents and abilities are God-given, for the purpose of serving Him.

In Acts 10, the apostle Peter visited the home of a Gentile named Cornelius. Cornelius was so overwhelmed by the honor that he fell down and started worshiping Peter. The apostle quickly pulled him to his feet and said, "Stand up! I'm a human being just like you!" (Acts 10:26 NLT).

Peter wanted no part of the glory that was due to God alone. He knew exactly what he was—and wasn't. That's why he was so useful to the Lord. And if we recognize the same about ourselves, we can be useful to Him as well.

### PRAYER:

*Holy God, You alone deserve glory and honor.*
*Let me never lose sight of that. In Jesus' name, amen.*

# GET WISDOM

*Joyful is the person who finds wisdom, the one who gains understanding. For wisdom is more profitable than silver, and her wages are better than gold. Wisdom is more precious than rubies; nothing you desire can compare with her. She offers you long life in her right hand, and riches and honor in her left. She will guide you down delightful paths; all her ways are satisfying. Wisdom is a tree of life to those who embrace her; happy are those who hold her tightly.*

PROVERBS 3:13–18 NLT

When Solomon succeeded his father, David, as king of Israel, God made him an extraordinary offer. Anything Solomon requested—wealth, long life, wisdom—God would grant him. Solomon chose wisdom, the ability to make wise choices in leading God's people. God was so pleased by Solomon's choice that He gave him untold riches and fame as well.

The reason Solomon's story still matters is that people face the same choice today, albeit in less dramatic circumstances. Almost everyone has the option of pursuing wealth, long life, or wisdom, not to mention fame, comfort, entertainment, security, peace of mind, and respect.

And strong cases can be made for each option. Yet as Solomon counsels from the pages of the Old Testament, wisdom is still the best bet. Wisdom allows people to apply what they know in ways that benefit themselves and others— and not necessarily in that order. Wisdom helps people understand and apply Scripture. Wisdom allows people to use their God-given gifts in extraordinary ways.

What's more, as Solomon discovered, God rewards the pursuit of wisdom. He may not lavish wisdom seekers with wealth and fame, as He did Solomon, but He will allow them to experience such intangible perks as peace of mind, security, and respect.

## PRAYER:

*Heavenly Father, thank You for Your generosity in giving wisdom to those who ask. Create a constant hunger in me for that wisdom. In Jesus' name, amen.*

# AGAINST ALL ODDS

*We may boldly say: "The Lord is my helper; I will not fear."*

**HEBREWS 13:6 NKJV**

Throughout Scripture, the people of God are challenged to be "bold." In I Kings 18, we're given a snapshot of boldness in action. Elijah was a prophet of God during an era when such a calling was highly unpopular. The evil royal couple Ahab and Jezebel had done everything in their power to wipe out the prophets of God so that their own prophets of the false gods Baal and Asherah could reign supreme.

Elijah proved to be a formidable opponent, however. In fact, he challenged the representatives of Baal and Asherah to a winner-take-all contest. The rules were simple. Two sacrificial altars would be built: one to the Lord God and one to Baal. The first deity to send fire to accept his sacrifice would be declared the God of Israel.

On the appointed day, 850 prophets of Baal and Asherah assembled to prepare their altar and sacrifice. When everything was just so, they began to pray to their gods to accept their sacrifice. They begged and pleaded. They cut their flesh to prove their faithfulness. They got nothing. Not even a slight warming of their altar.

Elijah alone represented the Lord God. One against 850. The 850 never stood a chance.

Elijah prepared his altar and sacrifice. He dug a trench around the altar. He recruited onlookers to fill large jars with water and pour it over his sacrifice. Jar after jar doused the altar until the water filled the surrounding trench.

Practically speaking, nothing on earth should have been able to ignite Elijah's sacrifice. The prophet of God prayed, "O Lord, God of Abraham, Isaac, and Jacob, prove today that You are God in Israel and that I am Your servant" (I Kings 18:36 NLT).

Fire descended from heaven to devour the sacrifice, as well as the altar, the dust, and the water in the trench. The impact was immediate and profound. "And when all the people saw it, they fell face down on the ground and cried out, 'The Lord—He is God! Yes, the Lord is God!'" (I Kings 18:39 NLT).

As long as people need that same reminder, the story of Elijah will still matter.

### PRAYER:

*I need no reminder: You alone are God. You alone are deserving of my praise and worship. In Jesus' name, amen.*

# KING OF PAIN

*In His kindness God called you to share in His eternal glory*
*by means of Christ Jesus. So after you have suffered*
*a little while, He will restore, support, and strengthen you,*
*and He will place you on a firm foundation.*

I PETER 5:10 NLT

If everything good in your life was suddenly taken away, would you remain faithful to God? That question lies at the heart of the book of Job.

Job was a righteous man—so above reproach that God held him up as a model of righteousness to Satan. Satan was unimpressed. "Of course he's faithful to You," he countered. "He has wealth, family, and excellent health. Take away those things and let's see how faithful he is."

God agreed to Satan's challenge. He allowed the devil to bring tragedy and suffering into Job's life. First came messengers with news that all of Job's flocks—the primary source of his wealth—had been stolen or killed. Next came news that all of Job's children had been killed in a storm. And then came the boils—painful skin infections that covered Job from head to foot.

Job was in agony, emotionally and physically. Yet he stayed faithful, much to the disgust of his spouse. "His wife said to him, 'Are you still trying to maintain your integrity? Curse God and die.' But Job replied, 'You talk like a foolish woman. Should we accept only good things from the hand of God and never anything bad?' So in all this, Job said nothing wrong" (Job 2:9–10 NLT).

Job wrestled with his situation, trying to reconcile his suffering with what he knew about God. He debated friends who blamed him for his misery. He held on to his relationship with the Lord—sometimes just by his fingernails. And when Satan's period of testing was over, God restored Job's health and wealth and blessed him with a new family.

Job walked the path through the valley of darkness that was laid out before him and emerged with God's blessing on the other side. The book that bears his name is intended for anyone who desires to do the same in their season of suffering.

### PRAYER:

*Father, thank You for walking with me through the darkness and the light. Give me the wisdom to see beyond my immediate circumstances and recognize Your never-ending care for me. In Jesus' name, amen.*

# THE LURE OF COMPETITION

*James and John, the sons of Zebedee, came over and spoke to Him. "Teacher," they said, "we want You to do us a favor. . . . When You sit on Your glorious throne, we want to sit in places of honor next to You, one on Your right and the other on Your left." . . . When the ten other disciples heard what James and John had asked, they were indignant.*

MARK 10:35, 37, 41 NLT

This passage offers a rare glimpse into the working relationship of the disciples. Specifically, James and John's audacious request reveals the competitiveness that existed among them. The "Sons of Thunder," as Jesus called nicknamed them (Mark 3:17), apparently saw themselves as more worthy of places of honor in Jesus' kingdom than their fellow apostles. The indignant reaction of the other ten suggests that their competitiveness wouldn't allow them to cede those positions to James and John without a fight.

Jesus nipped their petty one-upsmanship in the bud with

a few eye-opening comments about competitiveness. "You know that the rulers in this world lord it over their people, and officials flaunt their authority over those under them. But among you it will be different. Whoever wants to be a leader among you must be your servant, and whoever wants to be first among you must be the slave of everyone else. For even the Son of Man came not to be served but to serve others and to give His life as a ransom for many" (Mark 10:42–45 NLT).

Competitiveness—the drive to be better, faster, stronger, smarter, wealthier, more successful, and more obviously blessed by God than other people—tends to breed a me-centric approach to life that flies in the face of the true selflessness Jesus modeled. We can be the kind of servant Jesus calls us to be only if we refuse to view others primarily as competitors to be bested.

### PRAYER:

*Father, Your will for my life is all I seek—*
*nothing more, nothing less. Help me keep*
*my competitive urges in check so that*
*I can appreciate what You have in store for me.*
*In Jesus' name, amen.*

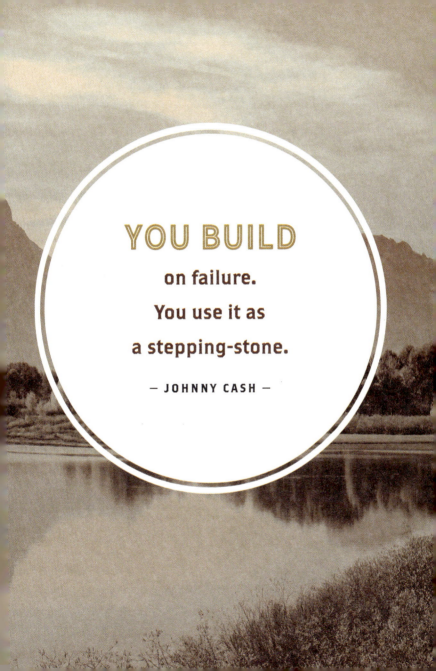

## YOU BUILD

on failure.
You use it as
a stepping-stone.

— JOHNNY CASH —

# BOUT WITH DOUBT

*Now faith is the substance of things hoped for,*
*the evidence of things not seen.*

HEBREWS 11:1 NKJV

**T**wo thousand years removed from the events of the Gospels, some of those "things not seen" seem hard to believe.

Guess what? They were hard to believe two thousand years ago as well.

According to John 20:24, Thomas was absent when Jesus first appeared to His disciples after His resurrection. When the others tried to share the good news with him, Thomas scoffed: "Unless I see in His hands the print of the nails, and put my finger into the print of the nails, and put my hand into His side, I will not believe" (John 20:25 NKJV).

The next time Jesus appeared to His disciples, Thomas was present. Jesus offered His wounded hands and side for closer examination. Thomas's doubt dissipated with a single breathless exclamation: "My Lord and my God!" (John 20:28 NKJV).

Doubt isn't necessarily the opposite of faith. Sometimes it's the precursor to faith. Genesis 1:27 emphasizes that humankind was created in God's image. One of the ways our likeness manifests itself is in our ability to think and reason, based on our experiences and interaction with the world around us. Therefore, when people are asked to accept something that defies reasoning or the laws that govern this world, they *should* wrestle with it—weigh it against what they know of this world and especially what they know of God.

The telling detail in this story is that Jesus didn't punish or shame Thomas for his doubt. Instead, He equipped him with the evidence he needed to believe. God does the same for us when we come to Him with our sincere doubts. He remains patient with us and works in us to shore up our belief.

### PRAYER:

*Father, I believe; help my unbelief.*
*You know the areas in which I struggle with doubt;*
*please help me work through them.*
*In Jesus' name, amen.*

# SPEAKING TRUTH TO POWER

*"Woe to you Pharisees, because you love the most important seats in the synagogues and respectful greetings in the marketplaces. . . . And you experts in the law, woe to you, because you load people down with burdens they can hardly carry, and you yourselves will not lift one finger to help them."*

**LUKE 11:43, 46 NIV**

Pharisees and religious leaders occupied a prominent place in first-century Jewish society. These teachers were revered for their wisdom and piety. Their words were treated as spiritual law by the people of Israel.

Their influence extended beyond the religious realm. They enjoyed a measure of political power, even though Israel at that time was ruled by the Roman Empire. The Pharisees and their ilk had the ear of Roman officials, who recognized the wisdom of supporting and facilitating Jewish religious practices and traditions.

To challenge or oppose the Pharisees, then, was to make some powerful enemies. Jesus certainly understood that. He knew which way the prevailing political winds blew. Yet He also recognized how power had corrupted Israel's religious leaders. He saw their vanity and hypocrisy.

The Gospels record several encounters between Jesus and the Jewish religious leaders of His day. But few are as pointed as the one found in Luke 11. After a Pharisee challenged Jesus for not obeying a tradition that had been accepted as religious law, Jesus launched into a scathing indictment of the greed, egotism, hypocrisy, and misplaced priorities that colored everything the Pharisees said and did.

The repercussions for Jesus' boldness would soon follow. The religious leaders were not people to endure chastisement—no matter how richly it was deserved—with grace and humility. They mustered a weak public defense of their actions. In private, though, they began to conspire against Jesus in more sinister ways. They discussed plans to rid themselves of this nuisance from Nazareth once and for all.

By then, though, the example had been set. By daring to speak out against those who abuse their authority, Jesus gives a voice to everyone who follows Him and encourages them to do the same.

Obviously, no one can speak with Jesus' moral authority. But His people can—and should—follow His example of speaking truth to power. Boldly. Fearlessly. Prayerfully.

### PRAYER:

*Father, Your truth trumps all human knowledge. Give me the courage to proclaim and defend it, regardless of who opposes me. In Jesus' name, amen.*

# YOUR SERVE

*Whoever wants to become great among you must be your servant, and whoever wants to be first must be slave of all. For even the Son of Man did not come to be served, but to serve, and to give His life as a ransom for many.*

MARK 10:43–45 NIV

On the night He was betrayed, Jesus stunned His disciples by filling a basin with water, draping Himself with a towel, and kneeling before them to wash their feet. Once they recovered from the shock of what they were seeing—their Master in a servant's pose, preparing to wipe the dirt and grime of the day's travels from their feet—they began their objections.

"You shall never wash my feet" Peter said (John 13:8 NIV). His point was clear: Such a menial, thankless act of service was far below One such as Jesus.

Only it *wasn't* below Jesus—and by extension, it isn't below His followers.

*When He had finished washing their feet, He put on His clothes and returned to His place. "Do you understand* what I have done for you?" He asked them. "You call Me 'Teacher' and 'Lord,' and rightly so, for that is what I am. Now that I, your Lord and Teacher, have washed your feet, you also should wash one another's feet. I have set you an example that you should do as I have done for you. Very truly I tell you, no servant is greater than his master, nor is a messenger greater than the one who sent him. Now that you know these things, you will be blessed if you do them." *(John 13:12–17 NIV)*

When God came to earth in human form, it wasn't to bask in people's adoration. He didn't come to enjoy the privileges and trappings of His exalted position. He came to serve, to lower Himself to the bottom rungs of human society and work to meet the needs He saw there.

And He calls His people to follow Him down. Jesus doesn't offer believers the luxuries of pride and selectivity. He understands that the acts of service that require the most sacrifice on the part of believers are the ones that speak most loudly to the world.

## PRAYER:

*Father, I stand amazed at the humble service of Your Son. Bless my efforts to follow His example. In His name, amen.*

# ALIVE

*He is not here, for He has risen, just as He said.*

**MATTHEW 28:6 NASB**

**H**e *has risen.* Those three words explain the startling condition of Jesus' grave on the very first Easter morning. The faithful women who had come to tend to Jesus' body two days after it had been entombed were distraught to find the tomb empty. Angelic messengers assured the women that no one had stolen Jesus' corpse—that, in fact, there was no corpse at all.

*He has risen.* With those three words, the darkness of Good Friday was lifted. Sadness and grief were abated. The power of death was broken.

*He has risen.* Upon those three words, Christianity was built. According to Scripture, two enemies stood between humankind and God: sin and death. Jesus defeated sin by living a blameless life before God and then offering Himself as a perfect sacrifice to pay the penalty for sin.

He defeated death by giving up His life on the cross, going into the grave as a corpse, and emerging two days later as the living, breathing Savior—the bridge between God and His human creation.

The apostle Paul emphasized the importance of Jesus' resurrection in stark terms: "If Christ has not been raised, our preaching is useless and so is your faith. . . . And if Christ has not been raised, your faith is futile; you are still in your sins. Then those also who have fallen asleep in Christ are lost. If only for this life we have hope in Christ, we are of all people most to be pitied" (I Corinthians 15:14, 17–19 NIV).

The good news—the best news of all, in fact—is that the events of the first Easter render those considerations moot. Jesus *has* been raised from the dead. And as the apostle Peter made clear, His resurrection makes possible the resurrection of everyone who follows Him.

"Praise be to the God and Father of our Lord Jesus Christ! In His great mercy He has given us new birth into a living hope through the resurrection of Jesus Christ from the dead, and into an inheritance that can never perish, spoil or fade. This inheritance is kept in heaven for you" (I Peter 1:3–4 NIV).

### PRAYER:

*Heavenly Father, thank You for the power of the resurrection. Because Jesus lives, I will one day live with You. In Jesus' name, amen.*

# A TIME OF REFRESHING

*Repent, then, and turn to God, so that your sins may be wiped out, that times of refreshing may come from the Lord.*

ACTS 3:19 NIV

I f *refreshing* seems like a surprising word to find in a verse about repentance, think about the emotional weight of guilt and shame. And think about the opportunity to be free from the turmoil they cause.

The words of Acts 3:19 have the power to change lives—immediately and forever. To fully appreciate that power, you must first forgive yourself. "Forgive and forget" is an easy thing to say. Yet forgetting can be difficult when the consequences of your sin—whether it's a broken relationship, a damaged reputation, or a destructive personal habit—are never far from your mind.

The thing you need to understand, however, is that those things are far from *God's* mind. How far? "As far as the east is from the west" (Psalm 103:12 NIV). If you've repented of a wrongdoing—no matter how serious—God will not hold it against you any longer. So unless you believe your standards are higher than His, there's no reason for you to hold it against yourself. Let it go.

One of the most insidious aspects of your sin is its damage radius. It rarely affects just you; it touches the lives of others, as well. Some people may be betrayed or hurt by your actions. Others may be influenced by them and tempted to follow your lead. Still others may be forced to reconsider their opinion of you. That's why repenting of sins involves making amends to people you've hurt.

Along those same lines, if you've embraced and internalized God's forgiveness, you'll be eager to pass it on to others. You'll want them to feel the freedom and excitement that comes from a fresh start. With some time, effort, and prayer, you'll learn to embrace the spirit of forgiveness found in Acts 3:19. You'll look at those who wrong you in a different light. You'll see yourself—or the person you *used* to be—in them. Where anger once dwelled, you'll find empathy.

### PRAYER:

*Father, thank You for forgiving and forgetting when I disobey You. Give me the courage to make amends with the people I hurt and the wisdom to forgive myself. In Jesus' name, amen.*

# OUR ADVOCATE

*I will ask the Father, and He will give you another Advocate,*
*who will never leave you. He is the Holy Spirit,*
*who leads into all truth.*

JOHN 14:16–17 NLT

When Jesus spoke these words, His disciples were struggling with the realization that He would leave them soon. Jesus helped them understand that their loss would soon be their gain.

Indeed, when the Holy Spirit came upon them at Pentecost several weeks later, their lives were changed forever. His power propelled them to unimaginable ministry opportunities and helped them tap in to resources inside themselves they didn't know existed. That same power is available to everyone who follows Jesus.

The Holy Spirit advocates on our behalf constantly. To fully understand His work, we must study His role in Scripture. Genesis 1:2 places Him at the center of the creation story. He also involved Himself in individual lives. In the book of Judges, He equipped Othniel (3:10), Gideon (6:34), and Samson (14:6) to fulfill their God-given responsibilities. Elsewhere He revealed God's truth to prophets (Ezekiel 2:2) and gave His blessing to Jesus' baptism (Matthew 3:13–17).

We must also consider His role in our lives. The Holy Spirit acts as our spiritual conscience, letting us know when we've done something wrong and urging us to repent. Pangs of guilt or regret are among the tools He uses to maintain an intimate relationship between us and our heavenly Father.

According to Jesus, the Holy Spirit also serves as an advocate—a counselor, a helper, One we can call on in times of trouble. He knows the solution to every problem, the motives and agendas of the people we deal with, what the future holds, what God has planned for our lives, and how we can accomplish God's will. And He stands ready to offer His divine knowledge, insight, and wisdom when we need it most.

The Holy Spirit also serves as a conduit for prayer, expressing things to God that are beyond our ability to convey (Romans 8:26–27). He gives us spiritual gifts and guides our use of them (I Corinthians 12:11). He assists us in understanding spiritual truths (I Corinthians 2:10–11). The Holy Spirit makes it possible for us to live the lives God has called us to live.

### PRAYER:
*Father, thank You for the gift of Your Spirit.*
*Keep me attentive to His voice. In Jesus' name, amen.*

# SEARCH ME

*Search me, O God, and know my heart!*
*Try me and know my thoughts! And see if there be*
*any grievous way in me, and lead me in the way everlasting!*

PSALM 139:23-24 ESV

David, the author of this psalm, is described in Scripture as a man after God's own heart. His plea in this passage makes it clear why he holds such a distinction. David desires an intimate relationship with the Lord, one free from obstacles and distractions. He's asking the Lord to do a full scan of his life and make him aware of things that could interfere with that relationship.

You can grow closer to the Lord by following David's lead. Invite the Lord to search the dark corners of your life for actions, attitudes, or thoughts that may interfere with your relationship with Him. First, clear your mind of distractions. Begin a dialogue with God with a single-minded purpose. Set aside your to-do list, your work pressures, and your family drama. If you have trouble creating a proper mindset, try reciting Psalm 139:23–24 over and over.

Open yourself to Him in prayer: your marriage or dating relationships, your friendships, your work habits, your church involvement, your financial decisions, your entertainment choices, and your spiritual growth. Ask Him to show you the areas that are ripe for change.

Listen carefully. In I Kings 19, God promises to make His presence known to His prophet Elijah. A succession of powerful phenomena then roar past the cave opening where Elijah is standing: a wind strong enough to destroy mountains followed by an earthquake followed by a fire.

Yet God doesn't make His presence known through any of them. Instead, He uses a gentle whisper. As soon as Elijah hears it, he pulls his cloak over his face in fear and awe. He recognizes God's gentle voice because he was listening for it. If he'd been expecting it to come in some loud, dramatic fashion, he might have missed it completely.

The lesson to be learned is that it's vital to keep your eyes and ears attuned to God when you pray. You never know when a gentle whisper or a nudge of your conscience or an idea will reveal something important to you.

### PRAYER:

*Search me, heavenly Father. Show me the areas in my life where You want me to change. In Jesus' name, amen.*

# YOUR ALL

*Love the Lord your God with all your heart*
*and with all your soul and with all your strength.*

### DEUTERONOMY 6:5 NIV

One word—*all*—elevates this passage to a lifelong challenge for believers. There are times when your heart pursues ungodly things. When your soul struggles to love anything. When your strength is exhausted by daily life.

The challenge, then, is marshaling every bit of your heart, soul, and strength for the Lord's service. To get a sense of how far your love for the Lord extends, ask yourself some tough questions.

*Does it end when it conflicts with your self-interest?*

Do you cut moral corners when there's an advantage to be gained? Do you put your own interests and well-being above others'? Do you ignore God's Word when it spoils your fun?

*Does it end when emotions take over?*

In the heat of the moment, do you ever react to people in less-than-honorable ways? Do you "take an eye for an eye" when you're wronged? Do you let your moods dictate the way you treat others?

*Does it end when temptation becomes too intense?*

Do you struggle with certain compulsions or addictions? Can you identify with the apostle Paul's lament: "I do not do the good I want to do, but the evil I do not want to do—this I keep on doing" (Romans 7:19 NIV)? Do you lose sight of God when you're chasing a certain feeling?

*Does it end when it puts you on the wrong end of certain issues or debates?*

Do you worry about being too closely identified with certain Christian causes? Do you fear the potential backlash and reaction if you made your Christian beliefs known? Do you stay quiet when you should take a stand?

*Does it end when tragedy or adversity strikes?*

Do you pull away from God when you lose someone close to you—whether through death or circumstances, such as a broken relationship? Do you hold a grudge against Him for bad things that have happened?

Once you get a sense of the "boundaries" of your love for God, you can, with His help, expand them so that eventually they encompass all your heart, all your soul, and all your strength.

### PRAYER:

*Father, I want to love You with all that is within me.*
*Help me reset my boundaries. In Jesus' name, amen.*

# CIRCLE OF INFLUENCE

*Now there were certain Greeks among those who came up to worship at the feast. Then they came to Philip, who was from Bethsaida of Galilee, and asked him, saying, "Sir, we wish to see Jesus."*

JOHN 12:20-21 NKJV

This brief encounter offers a snapshot of Christian witness at work. The passage doesn't explain how the visiting Greeks knew about Jesus. Perhaps they'd been told about Him by a friend, as was the case with some of Jesus' disciples.

The point is, word had reached them, and they wanted to encounter Jesus personally. That same dynamic is still alive and well two thousand years later. Spreading the Good News of Jesus is a matter of gradually expanding your circle of influence, increasing the number of people you interact with, and making spiritual connections wherever you can.

If your goal is to be purposeful in expanding your circle of influence and making a difference in the lives of as many people as possible, here are three ideas to get you started.

First, strive for meaningful conversations instead of settling for small talk. Aim for something deeper than surface topics. Master the art of drawing people out. Dare to ask personal questions when it's appropriate. Find ways to introduce Jesus or spiritual matters into your discussion without making other people feel uncomfortable.

Second, volunteer to work with young people. Take advantage of opportunities to make a positive impact in their lives. Earn their trust. Offer godly advice when appropriate. Be a guiding light for kids who may not have a lot of positive adult role models.

Third, show people that they matter. Conversations will reveal pertinent details about people's lives. Not only do you want to guard that information, but you also want to keep it fresh in your memory so that you can ask the right questions when you follow up. You can demonstrate a caring heart simply by remembering what's important to the people in your life.

You don't have to be an evangelist to make a profound difference in the lives of others. You can let them see Christ in you simply by taking a genuine interest in them.

### PRAYER:

*Heavenly Father, thank You for the opportunity to continually expand my circle of influence. Equip me to help everyone around me see Christ in me. In Jesus' name, amen.*

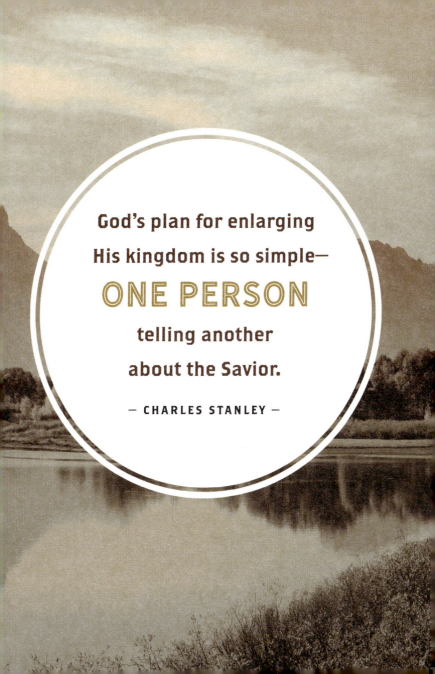

God's plan for enlarging His kingdom is so simple—

## ONE PERSON

telling another about the Savior.

— CHARLES STANLEY —

# A SERVANT'S HEART

*Do nothing out of selfish ambition or vain conceit.*
*Rather, in humility value others above yourselves,*
*not looking to your own interests but each of you to*
*the interests of the others. In your relationships with one*
*another, have the same mindset as Christ Jesus.*

**PHILIPPIANS 2:3–5 NIV**

The apostle Paul offers a unique opportunity and an extreme challenge to all followers of Christ. Rarely do believers get a chance to truly approximate Jesus' actions. Obviously, no one has His healing ability. No one possesses His wisdom. No one can speak with His authority. But with the right attitude and motivation, you *can* become a servant as He did. You *can* make a difference in other people's lives while maintaining a humble spirit.

You can do it by volunteering for ministry jobs no one else wants—low-profile, high-effort positions that often go unfilled. You can make a profound impact on your Christian community by volunteering to, say, teach a middle school Sunday school class or serve on a cleanup crew. Getting your hands dirty in ministry will help you discover the essence of Christlike service.

You can do it by deflecting glory. Jesus gave up His exalted position in heaven to come to earth. He emptied Himself of all the glory He deserved. His followers, then, have no reason to claim what He gave up. Resist the urge to draw attention to your ministry efforts, to "humble-brag" on social media or gain personal benefit from your work for God. When praise comes your way, deflect it to God, who makes your ministry possible and gives you the privilege of participating in His work. The best results come when you serve quietly, without fanfare, as Jesus did.

You can do it by encouraging others to pay it forward. The best Christian ministry is a gift that keeps on giving. That's why it's vital to encourage those who have been touched by your service to serve others. That's the ministry Jesus modeled. He changed people's lives and then encouraged those people to change other people's lives in His name.

### PRAYER:

*Father, thank You for the profound privilege of giving the gift that keeps on giving. Bless my ministry efforts so that You—and only You—receive the glory. In Jesus' name, amen.*

# MAKING PEOPLE
# GLAD THEY MET YOU

*And I have been a constant example of how you can help those
in need by working hard. You should remember the words of the
Lord Jesus: "It is more blessed to give than to receive."*

ACTS 20:35 NLT

The words of Jesus that the apostle Paul referred to in
this passage were far more radical than they appear. In
first-century Israel, wealth, power, and social standing were
viewed as gifts from God. The more you possessed, the more
blessed you were thought to be.

However, Jesus said if you want to experience real
blessings, use what you have—money, time, skills, energy,
resources—to help others. The best way to make life better
for yourself is to make life better for others.

You can start by studying Jesus' example. Jesus said, "I
have come that they may have life, and have it to the full"
(John 10:10 NIV). His purpose was to help others find their
purpose. To help them recognize their worth. To give them
opportunities to succeed. To meet their needs. To lend them a
hand in overcoming obstacles. He demonstrated through His
words and actions not just His love but also His willingness to

help. And He showed His followers how to do the same.

A willingness to help requires you to look around. When you're in a public setting, pay attention to the people around you. Notice their situations. Let their emotions and needs register with you. Learn to empathize by taking in as much information about others as possible.

Listen, too. The greatest gift many hurting and needy people will ever receive is a listening ear—someone who cares enough to enter their world, find out what's troubling them, ask questions, and get involved. Make a habit of striking up conversations with people you don't know. If you show genuine interest in what they say and who they are, you may become privy to their areas of need.

If you have the means to help someone yourself, volunteer your services. If not, find people who can. Work as an advocate for people in need. Come alongside them. Let them know that you're involved for the long haul. In short, make people glad they met you.

### PRAYER:

*Father, thank You for the awesome responsibility*
*of caring for others. Make me an instrument of Your healing.*
*In Jesus' name, amen.*

# BLOWING
# YOUR COVER

*Now Peter was sitting out in the courtyard, and a servant girl came to him. "You also were with Jesus of Galilee," she said.*

**MATTHEW 26:69 NIV**

On the night Jesus was arrested, His disciple Peter followed Him to the place where Jesus was put on trial for His life. Peter thought he was incognito until a servant girl noticed him in the courtyard. Her perceptive statement raises two important questions.

First, how do you get recognized as a disciple of Christ? Peter had been seen with Jesus throughout the region for three years. His Galilean accent also gave him away.

How might you be recognized as a follower of Jesus today? What actions and attitudes might give you away? These questions are important to consider because not everyone will be able to speak to you, to ask questions about your relationship with Jesus or the difference He's made in your life. But they can watch you.

Second, how should you respond to being recognized as a follower of Jesus? Peter panicked when the spotlight suddenly fell on him. Three times he denied even knowing Jesus. How might you respond in a similarly hostile environment? What if identifying yourself as a Christian meant subjecting yourself to people's anger, prejudices, and stereotypes? How can you respond in a way that honors God and resonates with others?

First, you can stand firm in your faith. Know what you believe and why. Don't allow yourself to be pigeonholed or stereotyped. Learn to defend your faith with humility, kindness, love, and empathy for people who oppose it.

Second, you can speak up for the truth. This means defending your faith in a way that communicates genuine love and concern for people. Christians are charged to "[speak] the truth in love" (Ephesians 4:15). Words spoken with humility and grace can ease tension and prevent conflict.

Third, you can go where others won't. Reach out to people who feel alienated from or angry toward the church. Help them understand that Jesus is the One we look to as our example, not other people. Be quick to share your struggles and weaknesses in the context of Jesus' strength. Establish a bond with people who are wary of Christians. Work to show them loving-kindness.

### PRAYER:

*Father, I want to be recognized as a follower of Your Son.*
*Help me make my discipleship apparent to everyone.*
*In Jesus' name, amen.*

# CULTIVATE GENEROSITY

*While Jesus was in the Temple, He watched*
*the rich people dropping their gifts in the collection box.*
*Then a poor widow came by and dropped in two small coins.*
*"I tell you the truth," Jesus said, "this poor widow has given*
*more than all the rest of them."*

LUKE 21:1–3 NLT

From a financial perspective, the widow's contribution was insignificant, a drop in the bucket compared to the offerings the rich people at the temple gave. From a spiritual perspective, the widow's generosity far surpassed that of her wealthier fellow worshipers. The fact that Jesus singles her out for praise drives home an important point: God does not want *x* amount of dollars from His people. He wants a generous, loving, faithful spirit.

You can cultivate that kind of spirit by counting your blessings. Look closely at what you have—not just your material possessions, but also your health, your skills and abilities, your friends and loved ones. Get a sense of all that God has given you.

You can cultivate a generous spirit by understanding

needs. Familiarize yourself with the work of various charitable organizations in your community. Find out whose lives they touch and how. Look for opportunities to use what you have—money, time, energy, skills—to assist them.

You can cultivate a generous spirit by thanking God for giving you a role in His plan. Participating in God's work with your generosity is like seeing your name in the credits of the greatest movie ever made. God's not asking you to give; He's offering you a role in His crew. Let gratitude be your primary emotion when you give.

You can cultivate a generous spirit by finding creative ways to stretch your gifts of money, time, skills, and energy. Instead of asking, "How much do I have to give?" try asking, "How much more can I give?" Brainstorm ways you can use unexpected financial gains to support a ministry initiative—or start a ministry of your own. Look for opportunities to put your skills and expertise to use in service to others who are in need. Be generous with your time and energy.

### PRAYER:

*Father, thank You for everything I have to give.*
*Let me use it in a way that pleases You.*
*In Jesus' name, amen.*

# PRAY WITH POWER

*Jesus went with His disciples to a place called Gethsemane. . . .*
*Then He said to them, "My soul is overwhelmed with sorrow to*
*the point of death. . . ." Going a little farther, He fell with His face*
*to the ground and prayed, "My Father, if it is possible, may this*
*cup be taken from Me. Yet not as I will, but as You will."*

MATTHEW 26:36, 38–39 NIV

Jesus felt the full weight of what was about to happen on the cross. So He turned to His Father for comfort, support, and reassurance.

You will never experience the extreme distress Jesus faced, but you will face your own dark nights of the soul. Times when the light at the end of the tunnel grows faint.

When you do, look to Jesus' experience in the garden for guidance. Pour your heart out to God. Give everything to Him and let Him work in and through your circumstances to bring ultimate good from them.

Start by praising Him for His work in your life. No matter how dire your situation is, beginning your prayer with praise and thanksgiving will set the tone for a conversation that pleases Him, helps you, and brings the two of you closer together. Recalling His past work in your life may also help ease your concerns about His ability to work in your current situation.

Acknowledge Him and His will as your top priority. Jesus concluded His plea with the words, "Yet not as I will, but as You will." He recognized the ultimate importance of God's plan being carried out to completion. Any other concern— even those involving personal comfort and security—are secondary. If you make a habit of ending your prayers with the same genuine request, you'll discover the peace and fulfillment that come from being part of God's will.

Pray for strength instead of escape. God's plan may not be to help you get out of a trying situation. He knows there's tremendous benefit in enduring hardship, walking through a proverbial fire, working through grief and pain, and coming out the other side. He may not give you an escape route, but He will give you the strength and will to persevere. And He will walk every step with you.

### PRAYER:

*Father, thank You for the awesome privilege and power of prayer. Your will be done. In Jesus' name, amen.*

# BEAR FRUIT

*I am the vine; you are the branches.*
*The one who remains in Me and I in him produces much fruit,*
*because you can do nothing without Me.*

JOHN 15:5 CSB

In the week before His crucifixion, Jesus was approaching Jerusalem with His disciples when He noticed a leafy fig tree in the distance. Hungry, He made His way to the tree, only to discover it bore no figs, only leaves.

"He said to it, 'May no fruit every come from you again!' At once the fig tree withered" (Matthew 21:19 csb). To His disciples' astonishment, Jesus cursed the tree for not producing fruit. It was not a horticultural lesson.

Bearing fruit is the very essence of the Christian experience. Jesus calls His followers to provide nourishment and sustenance to the world. The person who merely looks the part of a believer—one who says the "right" things, goes to the "right" places, and associates with the "right" people—is a leafy, fruitless tree. Beneficial to no one.

Unless you're "bearing fruit"—offering tangible evidence

of Jesus' work in your life—you haven't reached your full Christian potential. You can start that process by identifying your spiritual role models. Think about the Christians who have made a difference in your life. What character traits do they possess? What makes them stand out from other believers? What did they do to make a difference? Consider how you can follow their lead, using your own unique spiritual gifts and abilities.

Your goal is to make a difference in other people's lives. Personal improvement is one thing. But for fruit to be truly beneficial, it must provide nourishment and sustenance to others. Look for opportunities to get involved in the lives of people who need you, whether it's a young person without a positive adult role model, an elderly neighbor who's battling health issues, a friend going through a tough personal issue, or anyone else who could benefit from an encounter with a fruit-bearing follower of Christ.

## PRAYER:

*Heavenly Father, I want to provide nourishment and sustenance to others. Show me how to increase my yield. In Jesus' name, amen.*

# STAY ALERT

*Stay alert! Watch out for your great enemy, the devil.*
*He prowls around like a roaring lion,*
*looking for someone to devour.*

I PETER 5:8 NLT

After the Last Supper, Jesus asked Peter, James, and John to accompany Him to the garden of Gethsemane. The realization of what He was about to endure on the cross weighed heavily on Him. He wanted to spend some uninterrupted, one-on-one time with His heavenly Father, so He asked His friends to stay alert. His enemies were on their way to arrest Him.

His friends failed miserably in their task (Matthew 26:40–46). Three times they fell asleep while Jesus was praying. When they awakened the third time, they were surrounded by Jesus' enemies. The trio let their guard down just for a moment and found themselves overwhelmed by opposing forces.

The Bible warns that the same fate awaits believers who let down their guard today. Years after his failure in the garden, Peter wrote the verse quoted above.

The Bible makes it clear that Christians are foreigners in this world and, as such, should be prepared for opposition and oppression. We must maintain a heightened sense of alertness. We do that by understanding the importance of our task. Everything we say or do, every decision we make, reflects on Jesus. If we let our guard down, even for a moment, the results can be devastating.

We must eliminate distractions. The disciples were overcome with sleepiness. Their lack of physical preparedness was a distraction that affected their performance. Other distractions may include misplaced priorities, an overly busy schedule, or unresolved personal issues—anything that keeps us from serving Jesus to the best of our ability.

We must anticipate hot spots. We may not always be able to predict where an attack will come from, but we can get a sense of when conditions are right. Sometimes we can see the potential for temptation or conflict when we do certain things, go to certain places, or spend time with certain people.

We must let love guide our reactions when the heat is on. We must consider people's needs and situations before we respond to circumstances. We must find a way to make a difference in other people's lives without abandoning our own position.

### PRAYER:

*Father, thank You for entrusting me with a sacred duty.*
*Help me stay alert. In Jesus' name, amen.*

# LAMP AND LIGHT

*Your word is a lamp to my feet and a light to my path.*

PSALM 119:105 NKJV

In Psalm 119, the psalmist demonstrated not just a deep understanding of God's Word, but also a keen self-awareness. He recognized that daily diversions, temptations, and frustrations often cause us to lose sight of God's Word. He knew all too well the consequences of such a stumble. God's Word tethered him to God's will and kept him from pursuing his own ultimately self-destructive agenda.

For his own well-being, he vowed to give God's Word top priority in his life. If you'd care to embrace the wisdom of the psalmist, here are four things you can do to establish a solid connection with God's Word.

*1. Create a reading plan.*

The Bible can be explored in any number of ways. You may start with the story of Jesus in one of the four Gospels. You may study the letters of the apostle Paul. You may focus on one character at a time. You may look up passages related to a specific topic. Choose the option that best fits your needs and create a reading plan for yourself. If you don't know the Bible well enough to do it yourself, ask a church leader or mature Christian friend to help you.

*2. Establish a schedule.*

Set aside a specific time every day to spend in God's Word. Choose a time when your faculties are sharp and your energy is high. Once you've established a routine, guard your Bible study time zealously. Refuse to schedule anything else during that time.

*3. Keep a journal.*

Interact with Scripture in a tangible way. As you study God's Word, jot down your thoughts and ideas for applying what you read to your daily life. Ask questions that occur to you. Write down prayer requests, answers to prayer that you've received, and things for which you're thankful.

*4. Memorize.*

Each week or so, choose a verse or passage that has special meaning to you and commit it to memory. Repeat it to yourself until the words stick in your mind. Let it work in your life, giving you strength, comfort, encouragement, inspiration, and motivation.

### PRAYER:

*Father, I love Your Word. Be my lifeline as I explore its depths. In Jesus' name, amen.*

# WHAT ARE NEIGHBORS FOR?

*The second is equally important:*
*"Love your neighbor as yourself."*

**MARK 12:31 NLT**

In Mark 12:28–34, Jesus condensed the entire Old Testament law into two commands. The first, "Love the Lord your God," is relatively easy. God is eminently lovable. Doing a quick inventory of the blessings in your life is enough to inspire loving gratitude.

The second commandment, "Love your neighbor as yourself," is more problematic. For one thing, not all neighbors are inherently lovable. Some are petty. Some are hostile. Some are quick to take advantage of others. All are decidedly imperfect, as are the believers trying to show a loving attitude.

Therein lies the second problem. Showing love to others doesn't always come naturally. Negative emotions, past experiences, unhealthy competitiveness, and other factors can make it difficult to genuinely love your neighbor.

The solution is to look to Jesus' example. He showed loving-kindness to the people who rejected Him. He looked past His neighbors' imperfections and saw their potential. He accepted people as they were, yet He encouraged them to become better. He forgave them. He stepped into their lives to bring them hope, joy, peace, and health.

You can follow Jesus' example by praying for God's assistance. Ask Him to help you see people as He sees them—to help you recognize their potential and value. Ask the Holy Spirit to equip you with the patience, understanding, and motivation to make a difference in the lives of your friends, coworkers, casual acquaintances, or fellow public transit riders.

You can follow Jesus' example by making the first move. Many people will be (understandably) suspicious of someone who comes on too strong or who seems too eager to get involved in their lives. Discernment, then, is key to effectively showing love to others. Start with small gestures—a friendly introduction or a cup of coffee together. Strike up casual conversations and listen carefully for hints involving more personal issues or needs.

You can follow Jesus' example by staying humble. Humility is an appealing personal quality, one that tends to draw others to you. When you show love to your neighbors, the more unpretentious you are, the better your love will be received.

### PRAYER:

*Father, You didn't call me to a life free from challenges. I will strive to love my neighbors; help me when I fall short. In Jesus' name, amen.*

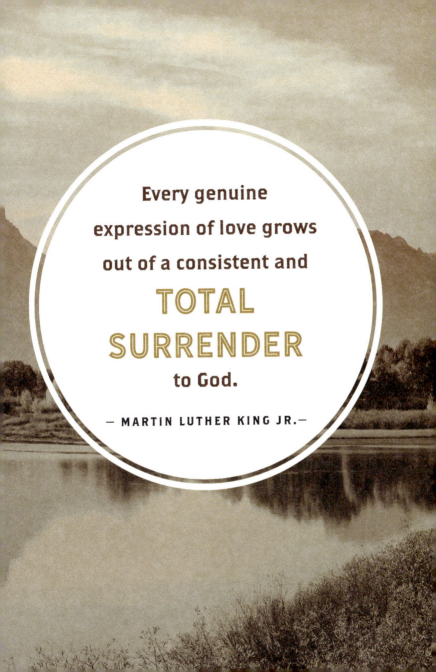

Every genuine
expression of love grows
out of a consistent and

# TOTAL
# SURRENDER

to God.

— MARTIN LUTHER KING JR. —

LIVE YOUR FAITH

*Dear Friend,*

This book was prayerfully crafted with you, the reader, in mind. Every word, every sentence, every page was thoughtfully written, designed, and packaged to encourage you—right where you are this very moment. At DaySpring, our vision is to see every person experience the life-changing message of God's love. So, as we worked through rough drafts, design changes, edits, and details, we prayed for you to deeply experience His unfailing love, indescribable peace, and pure joy. It is our sincere hope that through these Truth-filled pages your heart will be blessed, knowing that God cares about you—your desires and disappointments, your challenges and dreams.

*He knows. He cares. He loves you unconditionally.*

**BLESSINGS!**
**THE DAYSPRING BOOK TEAM**

---

Additional copies of this book and other DaySpring titles can be purchased at fine retailers everywhere.
Order online at <u>dayspring.com</u>
or
by phone at 1-877-751-4347